## Chapter 1

*Monday 25 September 2006*

'How quickly can you get him here?

'If I leave now it'll take at least twenty minutes.'

'Leave now,' he said.

I looked at Pablo Picasso, my handsome eight-week old kitten. He seemed fine. There were no signs of discomfort, his eyes were clear and bright, but Simon our vet told us this was common in the case of yew poisoning. Pablo may seem perfectly well until quite suddenly he would become ill and die.

The offending yew log rested by the fire, covered in leaves and the tell- tale chew marks of tiny teeth. I scooped up Pablo and placed him in his carrier, a wire mesh cage with an old pink towel at the bottom. He was used to the carrier and didn't struggle. His bright green eyes looked directly at me as I fastened him in, then he tucked his tiny paws underneath himself like a miniature black and white hen, relaxed and trusting.

'There's only one thing I can try,' said Simon when I arrived fifteen minutes later- a record for the journey between my home and the vet's practice in Whitby.

'I can inject him with something to make him sick. If there is any yew still in his stomach it could come up. If it doesn't, it may already be too late.'

Simon had told me to look out for any signs of drooling, vomiting, weakness or difficulty in breathing. The problem was that I didn't know exactly when Pablo had eaten the yew. I had cut the hedge that morning and brought a couple of short thick branches into the house to dry near the wood burner. It never crossed my mind that a cat might want to eat them. I'd gone out for a couple of hours and when I returned the awful evidence was before me.

Simon injected my tiny kitten and we waited. Nothing happened. After a few moments Pablo closed his tiny eyes, yawned, then keeled over sideways as though a hammer had hit him.

'What's happened to him' I asked, alarmed.

'It's a sedative, so his sleepiness is expected,' said Simon.

Pablo Picasso had the unconscious look of a cat that was not about to vomit. Slowly however, he began to stir, his third eyelid slid back and his eyes struggled to focus. His tiny sides began to quiver and we helped him to a standing position. He began to heave and his green eyes stretched wide in surprise as a dollop of fluid shot out of his mouth and onto the examination table. There was no sign of any yew leaves however.

'Are you sure he actually swallowed any?' said Simon.

I wasn't, I just didn't want to take the risk.

Pablo heaved again. His fragile ribs rose and contracted like small bellows - more fluid, no yew.

Exhausted by his ordeal Pablo sank back onto the examination table and let sleep overtake him. His mouth fell slightly open to reveal the salmon pink of his tiny tongue.

'It's up to him now.' said Simon. There was nothing more he could do. With luck, I hoped that Pablo had swallowed none of the poisonous leaves. I lifted him gently into his carrier being careful to support his head. When we got back to the car I looked across at him as he lay in deathlike sleep. His body was mostly black, but he had a distinctive stripe along his nose that split into two white flames that curled up towards his eyes. His front paws were as white as washed socks, and his back legs wore long white stockings. He also had thick white whiskers which gave him an intelligent, oriental look. In more relaxed times those whiskers were comical, now I just hoped it wasn't the last time I would see that wise old Confucius look.

Once I got him home and by the fire Pablo began to move as though dreaming he needed to get somewhere urgently. He opened his eyes and tried to work his legs which didn't seem to respond. Was this the poison taking hold? I helped him to stand and the heaving began again. He made an odd little squeak of discomfort and threw up again. This time four perfectly intact yew leaves lay on the newspaper I had placed underneath him. I dabbed them up with kitchen paper. Four yew leaves would have been enough to give him a premature and painful death. He

5

heaved again. One more leaf joined the four. Pablo made a noise that was a cross between a wheeze and a whistle, as though saying, 'Wow, did you see that?' Then he slumped back into sleep where he stayed for the next two hours breathing and whistling softly through his nose.

When he awoke the world was clean and new. He sat up, looked around himself and calmly took everything in as though he had just been born, which in a way was true. One life had ended and another begun.

## Chapter 2

My journey towards finding Pablo Picasso, his brothers and sister in a run-down area of Hull began in the summer of 2001, five years before Pablo was born. I was single and in my late thirties, a recent casualty of a failed marriage. I left the home I had known for years and rented a static caravan for the summer while I looked for a house or a flat - anything I could afford in the beautiful area around Whitby on the North Yorkshire Coast. Famous for Dracula and Captain James Cook I had lived in or near the town almost all my life. I loved the quaint old streets, the clear wide skies and the miles of golden sand.

I viewed tens of houses but I couldn't afford any of them. I looked at a couple of tiny one bed cottages down cobbled yards in Whitby where seagulls scolded like Victorian fishwives. The only people who could afford these places were those looking for a holiday bolt hole or a cottage they could let out to tourists and were for sale complete with crockery and bed linen. I looked in the villages along the valley of the Esk river. One of these was Kingfisher Cottage, a place with its back to the sun, a smell of damp and several holes in the roof. Even without paying for the work to put this right it was beyond my purse. I saw another tiny place advertised for sale by auction. It had a coffin sized garden, a kitchen the size of a walk in wardrobe and a lounge where you couldn't swing a mouse. Within the first three bids my faint hopes were dashed. Prices were increasing at a frightening rate and most rents were also out of my reach. I began to wonder whether I would have to get used to the nomad's life. While it was wonderful to sit outside a caravan in the sunshine at the bottom of a farmers field during the summer, I knew it would be a different matter to come home after a day's work, take a shower in the farmer's outhouse, fiddle with freezing gas bottles, light the fire and cook my miserable tea on two gas burners while I watched the condensation run down the inside of my windows.

The smart market town of Deyton was a forty minute drive away and houses there were more affordable. I decided the only thing to do was widen my search to include this area. I told the estate agents what I was looking for; something with a garden, a couple of bedrooms and I didn't mind a bit of work. I reckoned that if I had a spare room and things became really bad I could take in a lodger. Foulton and Harker's called me soon afterwards with the suggestion of a red brick townhouse on the Deytongate road. I drove across the North Yorkshire Moors from Whitby one late summer morning, when honeysuckle and ripening hawthorn berries were drying in the morning dew and the last of the purple heather let loose a cloud of honey scent into the warming air.

First I walked around the streets near the house, wandering into orchard fields and admiring the huge solitary trees and the network of well-worn paths I decided I could use for my morning jog. The railway station was a ten minute walk away, with a direct connection to York, and the main street was a two minute stroll; so far so good.

I approached Field House up a short flight of steep steps through a garden of groundsel and dandelion. The agent had told me that the owners, a Miss Flint who was a lady in her eighties and her brother of a similar age, had decided to carry out some work to the house but had run into difficulty.

Miss Flint greeted me in a soft, glad voice as though I was an old friend. First we walked out into the garden where sunlight washed over tufts of rose bay willow herb and glinted from the windows of the sturdy shed. A high sandstone wall glowed warm apricot. Without seeing anything further I was enchanted.

When we returned inside I began to see what a state the house was in and tried in vain to engage a sensible head.

'I can't seem to get round to finishing it,' said Miss Flint, wisps of white hair optimistically curling upwards. 'I pulled all the wallpaper off by myself and now I haven't the energy to redecorate.' Her legs were thin as kindling and her hands fluttered at her throat. Miss Flint's brother sat at the oak table, which rocked on the bare concrete of the kitchen floor. He peered hard through his thick rimmed spectacles into the workings of a ruined manual sewing machine.

'You took on a challenge.' I said to Mr Flint, but he didn't seem to hear me. Miss Flint moved me to the hallway which was scattered with curls of sawdust.

'He's lost his way,' she said quietly. 'Doesn't know if he's on his earth or Fuller's.'

I nodded. So Miss Flint had taken on the improvement of the whole house on her own and was also keeping an eye on her brother; no wonder she was struggling.

We climbed upstairs, past walls of crumbling plaster, into three cool bedrooms which smelled faintly of hay and roses. From the upper back window I could see over the top of the high sandstone wall at the end of the garden and into the grounds of the adjacent Old Manor Hotel. The sun cast deep shadows across the well-tended lawns through the branches of oak and horse chestnut and I noticed a grey cat pick a dainty path towards a warm brick wall where it licked a paw and curled up to sleep.

When we returned to the bottom of the stairs we could see Mr Flint standing on a kitchen chair peering into a high cupboard.

'Get down Jim, there's nothing you need in there,' said Miss Flint with gentle exasperation.

Mr Flint glowered down at us.

'Got to get the sheep shears ready,' he said, with agitated disdain.

'Sheep are all done, you did them yesterday, remember?' said Miss Flint.

Mr Flint looked at her with puzzlement.

'You sure?' he said

'Sure as I can be,' she said, 'now come down and get on with this Singer; I need it mended as quick as you can.'

We walked into the dining room, leaving Mr Flint to resume work on his hopeless machine.

'We used to keep sheep at Beadling. Farmed there sixty years.' she explained.

The dining room was lined with four enormous mahogany wardrobes and the floor was covered with small rugs, paintings stacked up and sheets draped over it all to air off like gypsy washing. There was no way of examining the walls or floor in here or for that matter in the lounge, which was stacked high with boxes, piles of paper, several standard lamps with murky coloured shades, horse tack and small machinery including a miniature blue steam engine. It was impossible. Despite this I knew this was the house for me. I told her how much money I had. The lovely Miss Flint nodded for a moment or two as though sympathising with sad news and then held out a dry thin hand.

## Chapter 3

I moved into Field House on the afternoon of 31 October 2001
with one car load of belongings and a bag of sweets for trick or
treat. When I arrived Miss Flint was still in residence. She
appeared at the door holding a rough yard brush approximately
the same size as herself.

'Just giving her a last sweep down and we'll be off,' she said. I
looked down at the brush. There were a few autumnal leaves
caught in the bristles and more leaves and dust drifted lazily
about her feet in the breeze from the open door. Miss Flint wore
a thick tweed skirt and a long pair of oatmeal coloured knitted
socks which were so lacking in elastic that they stood out around
her legs. Above these, the lady of the house stood straight and
brittle, her white hair escaping from a head scarf and her face
tilted up toward me with a blue eyed look of benevolence. I
wanted to hug her for all her years of effort, for her care of Jim
and her good heart. Instead, I stepped into the hallway and she
stood back to let me in. The new owner of Field House.

The building felt cold.

'Don't worry about the boiler,' she said.

I hadn't been worried until that moment.

'It's been absolutely fine, until just this morning, and then it
started to jip a bit.'

'What do you mean, *jip a bit*,' I said

'Well she seems to have stopped working just for the time being,' she said, and shook her head indulgently as though the boiler were a naughty child she could make nothing of.

'Well, never mind. I'll see to it,' I said.

'Yes, yes, I told Jim you'd soon have it licked into shape.' She said this with such conviction I almost believed I could mend it there and then.

I helped her carry their few remaining bags to a beaten up old Ford, helped Mr Flint into the passenger seat with the promise of a sheep sale, and then waved them off to their new life in a bungalow on the other side of the river.

Once they had left, the house felt empty and sad. There were areas of exposed brick and great cracks in the remaining plaster. The floors were bare boards in the two living rooms and sloping concrete in the kitchen. The windows in the dining room stared bleakly onto the street. For a moment I doubted whether I had made the right decision on that sunny late summer day.

I hung a set of charity shop curtains, lit the fire, put on the kettle to make myself a warming drink. Then I erected my blue fold up garden chair and sat in the Flint's home feeling lonelier than I had felt since leaving my husband. I wondered if I could ever make this place feel like home.

## Chapter 4

Though it had come out of sadness the next year was a time of discovery and unexpected moments of happiness. I discovered a knack for decorating and was lucky to find Mark, a reliable builder to complete the work I couldn't do. Mark was a man with a young family just beginning his business. He was meticulous in his work. He cleaned up after himself and sometimes redid work he wasn't satisfied with. I came home one day to find him washing all the plates in my cupboards because of the dust from his stone saw! He opened up the fireplace in the lounge, installed a sturdy Farndale stove from Moorland Fires in Beadling, took paintwork back to the original wood and oiled it until it shone. Each room was re plastered and I painted them in fresh light colours. Mark levelled the old sloping concrete floors and arranged for a rather stately and gleaming kitchen to be fitted where the rusted gas stove and Mr Flint's old table had stood before.

It felt like company to get home from work, turn on the radio and get out the paint brushes. The house had become a friend that grew more handsome every day. Mark kept an eye on house prices during this year and we saw the building bloom into what he called a 'lovely example of an Edwardian town house.'

During the spring of 2002 I began to notice a slender grey queen cat visiting the garden. She would sit by the wall watching me as I dug up the weeds. Every weekday I would leave the house for my work in Hull at seven thirty and be back by six. After a week or two I noticed that the little cat would appear in the garden as soon as I arrived home and stand by the back door looking up expectantly. I never let her into the house, and certainly never gave her anything to eat, because I knew how cross her owner would be if I did that. However, one night I was woken up by the sound of the dustbin lid crashing to the ground and I ran downstairs to see the grey cat cowering at the back of the garden. Another morning I found the bin lid had been silently tipped off and the liner was ripped apart with the remains of a chicken carcass strewn about the garden. A chicken carcass meant bones and I was worried that the grey cat had eaten them which would have done her no good at all. My worry deepened when I didn't see her for a few days, but then she came back, her slightness now tending towards emaciation.

Who did she belong to? Whoever it was, they weren't looking after her very well. Her eyes seemed huge in her head, her face was gaunt and I could see the line of her ribs as she stalked about the garden. When she caught sight of me now, she came rushing towards me meowing as though we were old friends. It wasn't long before I started to leave food out for her and from here it was a short step to her taking up residence with me at Field House. She came in as though she owned the place and a part of me wondered whether kind Miss Flint had been feeding her too. If so, it had taken me a long time to get the hint. I took my new feline friend to the vet who checked for an identity chip. There wasn't one. She was malnourished but other than that she was well. The vet estimated her age at about two years old.

'Looks like you've got yourself a cat,' the vet said. When I took her home the little cat trotted to the stove and curled up in front of it, and that was that, we were officially cat and owner. Of course, I knew as well as anyone that nobody ever actually owns a cat, but from that day on she allowed me to pretend that I did.

I called my cat Gracie May. It suited her gracefulness. Gracie May was a great companion through the spring and summer of house improving. I was able to work from home sometimes which meant I saved myself an hour of journey time each way. I could put in an hour of work on the house before I turned on the computer and then have an extended evening of decorating once the working day was over.

I improved the garden, which turned out to have wonderful soil. Back in the autumn I had ordered bare rooted David Austen shrub roses and three specimen standards. These now began to sprout new leaves. My geraniums flowered and an Elizabeth Montana clematis studded the front porch with hundreds of pink flowers. Every now and then I would treat myself to a cinema trip and revelled in 2002 releases such as The Bourne Identity, Bend it Like Beckham and The Road to Perdition, munching gleefully on popcorn and revelling in the well-earned rest. Sometimes my sister Clare would visit from Edinburgh and give me a hand, or my friend Kate would come over from Scarborough and paint woodwork with me while we listened to Desert Island Discs. My father took on the task of tiling my kitchen in a chequerboard of black and white. Gradually I noticed I felt less lonely. Gracie May had helped me feel that the house was now a home, but something else was happening that had nothing to do with her coming into my life. I was beginning to feel free.

## Chapter 5

I had to build up my courage to visit the local pub which was only a few doors down the road. I knew this would be a way to meet some of my new neighbours but I was nervous of going in on my own. I knew nobody at all in Deyton and save for waving at a friendly person who regularly walked past my window and the usual polite good mornings from passers-by, I had not improved the situation at all. I was rather a shy person, and didn't find it easy to let people know I was new and would appreciate a friend or two. I persuaded my friend Kate to come along with me. She was much more extrovert than I was and didn't think twice about turning a few heads. That first evening at the pub we met up with a group of people straight away. They were a very friendly bunch of six people who met at The White Horse every Friday to catch up with weekly news. They were an interesting mix of backgrounds and interests and all of them were single. A couple of women worked in the bank and lived on the other side of the river in Bourton. Another of the women had her own tepee making company. One of the men worked for an oil company in the Middle East and regularly spent weeks away from home, there was a plumber and then there was Henry, the owner of a stylish art gallery in the market square.

Henry and I hit it off immediately, I found him intense and rather exotic with his dark eyes and heavy brow. He wore ironed jeans and a yellow cravat and lay oddly in my imagination between a Bronte Heathcliffe and a Wodehouse Wooster. We were creatures from very different worlds but I soon discovered that there was something hypnotically attractive to me about Henry. All other faces faded into the background as we talked and talked. At last the pub lights flashed to tell us it was time to go. Kate blew me a kiss and disappeared out of the door.

'How will you get home?' enquired Henry, perfectly aware that I lived only a few paces from the pub door.

'I'm not sure unless you can think of someone who might walk me there.' I said, and held out my arm.

We reached my door approximately thirty seconds later. Henry smiled at me under the street light then took hold of my face in his hands as though examining a painting.

'You'll come and meet my race horse?' he asked.

Race horse?

'I'd love to,' I said and raised my hand in a short wave as he walked a few steps backwards, out of the circle of street light and off into the night.

The next week as we walked by the river, we realised we shared a love of romantic poetry and had both read Wordsworth's *The Prelude*. We talked of the poet's solitary wandering, of the vast frozen lakes and looming darkness of mountains. Another day we watched his race horse exercise on a beautiful frosted morning. She was all fire and spirit and her flanks shone in the sun. I visited his gallery which smelt of oil paint and polish and where the soles of my shoes squeaked across the shining floorboards.

We spent pleasant afternoons walking in the countryside around Deyton. It wasn't the harshly stunning moorland I knew and loved but the muted greens of the Wolds which were welcome and lovely.

One time we looked over a gate at the sheep in a field while Henry recited 'I leant upon a coppice gate,' the opening lines of Hardy's *The Darkling Thrush*. The poem, which was so much about hope, strangely seemed to create a sense of melancholy in us both and we were silent for a while, until I noticed that Henry was crying. It turned out he was in mourning for the loss of his marriage. He couldn't understand what had happened and was stunned by the fact of being alone. To make things worse, his mother had died the year before and he had been devoted to her.

Rather than draw us closer together this openness seemed to mark a change in Henry. Our conversations became more and more about himself than our love of literature or the countryside. Time after time I would return home to realise we hadn't laughed or smiled once. I was struck by how different he was from my ex-husband, Richard, who had been so aware of his own emotional landscape. Again and again Henry tried in his stilted and reserved way to tell me of his grief at his mother's death and of his incredulity at the ruin of his marriage in which he was apparently blameless. He proudly told me how his mother had been protective of him and had sheltered him from the harshness of what my parents would call the 'real world' of cooking, cleaning, paying the bills and doing things we didn't always want to do. She wanted him to keep his mind free for finer things.

He didn't have any experience of the rougher world I inhabited. When he visited me he would never think to put more coal on the fire, or help with washing up and I began to think he saw me as curious and a little too down to earth. He had limited understanding of the difficult circumstances many people lived in, the houses packed with three generations of a family, illness, neglect or financial hardship. Also, I couldn't find any trace of a practical skill in him. He seemed unfamiliar with the boundaries of his own physicality. His hands, for example moved hesitantly whenever I asked him to get to the other side of a piece of furniture to help move it or to pass me a knife in the kitchen. He bumped his head on corners and doors.

He loved taking his dog on ten mile runs where he could pound away his sadness. He often ate out alone in local restaurants. After a time he preferred to do these things than to walk with me. I recognised he was at the beginning of a long road to recovery, a road which didn't include me as a companion.

He told me I was becoming distant and I knew that it was true. After a few short weeks we agreed to part and I returned to my solitary life. I was shaken, but glad I hadn't missed out on our odd brief liaison.

 In my marriage I had been as much to blame as my husband Richard for the harsh words, misunderstandings and proud silences that gathered to a head in the last few months we were together. I could have listened more and taken less offence. In time Henry may have realised similar truths about himself and acknowledged the part he undoubtedly must have played in the breakup of his own marriage. Until then, it felt right to let him go.

## Chapter 6

My builder Mark and I had finished the work on Field House and I was proud of what we had achieved. Mark told me he thought I'd done a really good job, 'for a novice.' The whole enterprise had boosted my confidence and I listened with interest when Mark told me he was buying up cheap property to do up and rent out or sell on. Although I wasn't skilled at building he convinced me that if I could raise the capital for a deposit there was no reason why I couldn't buy a place and join the growing hordes of buy to let landlords. I began to read books on 'buy to let' and wondered if I, without any prior experience, would be capable of increasing my housing stock by one. Mark thought I should give it a go. Another friend however advised me to stick with what I knew and that people lost a lot of money when they paddled out of their depth.

My family had never been business minded and my parents had always been fairly risk averse, so it took a great deal of courage to contemplate an investment of my own. My job was not well paid but it was fairly secure so I reckoned I stood as good a chance of making a success as anyone.

To distract myself from the vacuum of long evenings alone and with Field House painted, carpeted, tiled and shining I had the place officially revalued and the mortgage company allowed me to release funds for a new deposit on a buy to let house. I considered my options and began to look in my work town of

Hull. There was one reason for this and one reason alone- it was the only place I could afford.

The centre of Hull is spacious and sophisticated, filled with museums, art galleries and bistro style eateries. The quays are bright with cutting edge architecture, vaulted glass and mirrored windows reflect the changing moods of the North Sea. The Humber Bridge is majestic and beautiful.

Hull has a long association with literary scholars. The Australian author Peter Porter described it as 'the most poetic city in England,' Philip Larkin set a number of poems there and the poet laureate Andrew Motion used to lecture at the University. In Hull, you can experience the curiously silent world of The Deep, an enormous underground aquarium with a staggering variety of marine life.

This Hull, the one you can read about in a brochure is not the Hull I knew. As I searched for my buy to let house I spent long and lonely lunch times and evenings trudging around the shabbier streets with lower price tags. I looked at houses on estates where it seemed that packs of roaming dogs were the only inhabitants. In my previous work in Scarborough I'd been no stranger to areas of poverty and hardship but it was nothing compared with what I began to think of as the Badlands. These were the areas the tourist information centres didn't mention, where billboards sagged from tired brickwork promising bright teeth, great hair and happy healthy children. People here had insufficient space and light, they couldn't afford decent food and the air was heavy with fumes and dust.

I often looked around these places alone thinking that if I felt nervous there was no way I should consider buying a house. There were many places I ruled out straight away and quite a few where I didn't even get out of the car. Yet I had to be realistic, I was on a tight budget and there was no safety net. An expensive house would mean a big monthly pay out and I didn't want to be caught paying two high mortgages without any rent coming in.

In Hull I became aware of a level of poverty I had only ever read about before; I talked with people desperate to sell houses they could not afford to keep, houses in narrow groves that looked directly across into the windows of their neighbours only feet away. I wandered down street after street strewn with rubbish, dog excrement, broken glass and where dirty faced children peered at me sullenly from street corners.

At last, in the winter of 2002 I found a house that felt right. It was a cut above the grubby little clusters of houses with front yards filled with burst mattresses and broken toilets. This street was tree lined and had a faint air of respectability. It was near a row of shops that had no bars up at the windows and where most of the dogs were on leads and had owners. Dellon Street cost me just under £30,000. I had spent weeks viewing some of the worst housing I had ever experienced, but in Dellon Street I felt I could make something work. The house had three bedrooms and a tidy back yard. The neighbours came out to chat with me and were friendly and proud of the way their street remained litter and trouble free.

I spent £200 on paint and tidying up the yard and found a letting agent, Alison, to help me find my first tenant. Alison approved of my choice; she knew the pitfalls of coming into the area with a wad of cash and buying the first cheap property with too little thought. I had paid for a survey up front and didn't buy the house until I knew it was sound. Alison told me that people were so keen to buy that they were bidding at auction on houses they hadn't seen and knew nothing about. She told me horror stories about black mould, subsidence and vandalism, people calling her in tears, police involvement and unsuitable tenants who would not budge.

'Remember it isn't a game and these houses are not sweeties in a shop window. Keep it real and you won't go far wrong,' she said.

Alison had a list of people waiting to rent a property like Dellon Street and within a month a new family moved in. It felt easy. My tenant paid on time and didn't bother me unnecessarily. The rent paid the mortgage with a little to spare.

Alison agreed to help me look for another property. If I could do it once I could do it again- right? Two houses were better than one, and after all, the market was still rising. I went out searching and when a new property caught my eye I contacted Alison and we viewed together. For a long time nothing suitable came up and the search became a protracted and exhausting business. I was viewing in my lunch hour, after work and at weekends. Friends were not keen to tramp around the less salubrious quarters of the city and I spent most of my time searching alone as I had before. I began to think it might be better to stick with what I had, but a few thoughts encouraged me to continue. I considered the potential in a rising market to sell up for a profit at some point in the future and pay a lump off what I owed on Field House. I was a late starter with a mortgage and I was looking at paying this off in twenty years' time, which felt to me like a life sentence. The days of even relatively well-off first time buyers unable to get a foothold on the housing ladder were not yet a reality and so I couldn't compare myself or feel privileged to be in the position I was. Another reason I carried on my search was the feeling that I was travelling into territory that was testing me, and for some reason that felt like a good thing. Also, my agent Alison was a strong and savvy woman who encouraged me.

Even in Hull prices were soaring. By the summer of 2003, just after my fortieth birthday, houses on Dellon Street has increased in price. They were now going for £50,000 which was £20,000 more than I had paid. I had to search hard to find a property I could now afford that was sound, in a reasonable area and which would also let out easily.

A house on Nancy Grove seemed to fit the bill perfectly. It was a smaller house than Dellon Street and was in one of those tight little cul- de- sacs with a narrow path separating each side of the street. Thankfully there were no mattresses in the yards and the end house was tucked safely away looking out over a field. It belonged to an elderly couple who had lived there all their married lives. They had brought up a family, their children had played in the field, and the husband had worked on the fish docks. They were quiet respectable people and I warmed to them and their home straight away.

I took Alison to look at it. She sat with me in a grubby coffee shop nearby after we had taken a good look around both the house and the streets close by.

'It's up to you of course,' she said, adjusting her skirt on the torn seating. 'But if it were up to me, I'd leave it.'

'It's all I can afford,' I said.

'I'd still leave it,' she said.

I bought it anyway.

I have no idea why I was stupid enough to ignore Alison's advice but she turned out to be right. I think it could have been as simple a reason as feeling tired of the search and impatient to get something up and running. Whatever it was I have had time at leisure to remind myself what a fool I was.

This house cost me £40,000. It wasn't until after I got the keys that I felt slightly uneasy at the razor wire on the garage roof or began to recognise that the field was less of a pretty feature and more of an area that potential thieves could use to access the roof. The green area turned out to be an old burial ground, grassed over, where big kids used to kick balls about, bully smaller kids and as I soon discovered, to light fires in old oil drums or against trees.

I now owned, or rather had mortgages on three houses and I needed to rent my latest house out quickly so that I could get some income. Rentals were not high on Nancy Grove. Most prospective tenants were claiming housing benefit and a number of people made appointments to view but didn't turn up. Alison told me she wouldn't deal with this house as the area was not in her preferred part of town. Ignoring my growing sense of foreboding I reassured myself that the house was solid and that it was tucked inconspicuously away. A polite couple had lived there safely all their married lives- what could go wrong?

As it turned out, rather a lot.

## Chapter 7

I was drinking coffee with my friend Kate in the garden of Field House. Gracie May sat on my lap as Kate and I talked about a recent narrow boat holiday we had enjoyed and how beautiful the canal had been between Wilmcote and Stratford Upon Avon. Kate had been suffering with a painful back during the holiday so she was on tea duty while I had attended to the locks. Nancy Grove, with its razor wire and litter was a long way from my mind.

At Field House I had cleared the brick path which led from the decked area where we sat so that it was visible all the way to the wall. The path was now lined with pots of bright colour and I had smartened up the shed and filled it with fuel so that every time I went inside I breathed in the aroma of drying logs. Today Kate and I caught the perfume of sweet peas on the lazy afternoon breeze. A buzzard made its mewing cry, high up, and we could see its heavy outstretched wings as it climbed the air currents.

'You know, you've done a good thing with this house, but you understand that this is not the end don't you?' she said.

'But I'm happy here. It's the way I want it,' I said.

'I know you're pleased now, but I'd be disappointed if when I visited you in two years time, you were still here,' she said. 'You belong back home.'

Since the house had been finished I had been ignoring a soft but insistent feeling of unease and until I heard those words I hadn't know what it was. Of course Kate was right. I had transformed Field House but sadly it didn't feel that I should stay. I realised that this place was meant to be a stepping stone to somewhere else; it was a place to cut my teeth and show what I could do. My heart had never really left Whitby and I wondered if there was any possibility I could afford to return to the area I loved so much. I missed the moorland, the miles of open sand and the sound of the sea. My other concern was that each time I parked up I would often find Gracie May waiting for me. This meant she had negotiated a busy main road to welcome me back. I witnessed her car- stopping methods of crossing the road with horror on more than one occasion and knew it was only a matter of time before a vehicle hit her.

Two years after I bought Field House I put it back on the market and by the autumn I had sold it to a lady artist who loved the light and spacious rooms, the profusion of roses and geraniums and the sandstone warmth of the walled garden. Though I sold Field House for twice what I paid for it this was still only sufficient to buy the tiniest cottage with one bedroom back home. Still, I had made moving back a possibility and I could afford to look at property in the beautiful North Yorkshire Moors National Park.

On an Indian summer day in September I made my way to the pretty village of Rilldale to view a gorgeous little cottage with beams, exposed floor boards and an open fire – the name alone made me love it even before I had laid eyes upon it.

Cat's Cradle.

From the kitchen window at Cat's Cradle I could see right down across the valley, over the roof tops of houses further down the village to Litton woods which lay under a mysterious cloak of mist, and beyond this again to the moorland on higher ground. It was perfect.

I was brought up with cats and always loved their independent yet affectionate natures. My first was a kitten rescued from a water trough at a riding stable – a scrawny mewling thing that grew up to be a sleek and glamorous she- cat called Tussy. Tussy was followed by Alexandra Pusskin, then a Zen cat named Norman who spent his days gazing into the middle distance.

Cat's Cradle seemed a very apt name for a house I would move into, particularly as I now had Gracie May - the new cat in the cradle.

Chapter 8

I moved into the cottage on 22 December 2003, on one of the bleakest, snowiest days of the year. The removal man phoned to check that the road between Deyton and Whitby was still open as it was often closed in snowy weather. I checked and found it was passable only with caution. I wondered if he was going to pull out of the agreement but he worked out of York, warmer by a couple of degrees than the road we would be travelling. Experience had shown me that it is easy to disbelieve reports of snow on high ground; you don't quite believe it until a blizzard is swirling into your windscreen. At Field House the wind whistled through the chinks in the windows and snow began to drift softly in the garden. Thin slush already covered the road outside the house. I knew that on the higher ground the roads would be growing treacherous. We had no time to waste.

The removal man arrived cheerful and untroubled and it took us less than an hour to pack my worldly goods into the back of the van. Just before we left I rushed upstairs to pick up Gracie May. She had settled happily into a basket and watched all the movement with unperturbed interest. Even when the police called in to tell me I was causing an obstruction she didn't seem at all phased. What else could I do? My house was on the road and there was no other way of getting my belongings into the removal van other than by parking it in a very inconvenient place. I apologised to the policeman, placed Gracie May in my little blue car on the passenger seat, dropped off the keys with the estate agent and set out from Deyton. The removal men followed me out of town and we completed the ten minute journey to Beadling with no mishap. At Beadling roundabout there was a neon display of the temperature which flashed up as we crossed the roundabout, - 1 degree centigrade.

As we drove out of Beadling the snow began to come down in huge flakes, sliding down the windscreen in wet blobs. The snow on the road was soft and fell into ridges at the sides. There were two dark tracks where previous tyres had been. The removal van behind me was going well. The road began to climb, and trees gave way to fields, we passed a pig farm and an open area of moorland where snow clung to the wire fences and blew across the road making drifts at each side. There was barely room for two cars to pass each other once we reached the top of Saltersgate. This area looked out over a great valley called the Hole of Horcum. Legend had it that a giant has thrown a huge boulder which had created a great impression. In summer, people came to fly model planes and to hang under microlights, but today there was only a steely sky and whiteness all around.

The snow came down faster in thin dry flakes which brushed the windscreen. The road now wound down towards a dangerous bend. Tracks from cars that had skidded veered off towards a broken fence. The powdery snow lay lightly on top of ice on the corner. I inched my way down while Gracie May peered out at all the wonderful brightness unaware of the danger. I felt the back of the car begin to slide round slowly like a skater on ice. Somehow I regained a grip and looked in my rear view mirror. The removal van was crawling along leaving space for me to get down first. The last thing they wanted was to spin out of control and end up ploughing into the back of my car.

Ahead I noticed a car that wasn't moving anywhere; it was stuck at the foot of a small slope, its wheels spinning. Further on there were men shovelling salt under the wheels of other cars, similarly stuck. These men were keeping the road open for the early warning station located in the middle of the moor. I pressed my foot a little harder on the accelerator; the wheels spun, then took hold of salt and moved forward. The removal van was close behind, making sideways progress up the incline. When we reached the turn off I would usually take through Grosmont to Rilldale I realised there was no way we could use it. The snow was piled in a great sweep like a frozen wave at the entrance to the turning and beyond it more snow lay thick and deep with no tracks. We carried on until eventually we reached the top of a hill and suddenly the snow stopped falling. It was as though we had emerged from behind a curtain. Here was a scrap of blue sky and a weak ray of sunshine illuminated an expanse of sea. As the road began to dip down, the fallen snow became softer, the blackness of the road showed through and we were over the worst.

However, we still had the steep Nimble Hill to negotiate into Rilldale village. I hoped that the piles of salt I had seen on previous visits had been put to good use, but I needn't have worried. Though the winding road to the top of the hill was covered with compressed snow and the way hemmed in by drifted waves of sparkling white, the top of the hill was generously scattered with dark salt which had bitten down to the tarmac. We drove down into the bottom of the village, past the ford, under the railway bridge, past three pubs, up to the top where at last we reached Cat's Cradle. We'd made it. A journey which would usually take around fifty minutes had taken us an hour and a half.

The previous owners had kindly lit a fire which was roaring up the back of the chimney. The room smelt of wet snow and coal dust. I found the kettle and the removal man and I stood in front of the fire for a few minutes to thaw out before dipping chocolate biscuits into large mugs of strong tea laced with Demerara sugar.

As I looked around I was reminded that Cat's Cradle needed work. Lots of it. The doors were falling off their hinges, the staircase was crumbling and I knew that the chimney stack sat at a rakish angle on a roof which was missing a number of tiles. There were no carpets anywhere in the house. The bathroom consisted of a tiny bath squashed down the short wall of the room and an old fashioned heavy toilet that rocked ominously. Of course, I couldn't afford three bedrooms or a beautifully presented house here in the National Park; in fact the only bedroom in Cat's Cradle had no door. Despite this I just had to look out of the window to remind myself how lucky I was. It was a vision from heaven. A crisp whiteness dazzled and stretched for miles. The removal man took off his hat and whistled. 'What a view!'

What a view indeed.

## Chapter 9

Gracie May was a pretty, unflappable cat. I kept her indoors for the first two weeks to let her get used to her new home. She spent hours with her nose inches from the glass in the kitchen watching the robins and blackbirds in the garden, calmly waiting for her chance to get out there.

That first Christmas at Cat's Cradle the rooms were deadly cold. No matter how high I stoked the open fire; as soon as I strayed from its heat the chill seeped in from the thick stone walls and froze my bones. I had blankets piled up on the bed and took a hot water bottle too and still my nose, the only part of me exposed to the air, was chilly. Gracie May lay on the pillow beside me, purring and keeping warm by curling up into a tight ball.

I bought a Christmas tree and decorated it with baubles I had gathered over the past couple of years. Some decorations I had made out of paper, little red heart shaped cups for holding a single chocolate, origami boxes and paper chains. I bought a string of coloured lights and draped them over the branches. The tree stood in the kitchen on the cracked bare tiles, with crepe paper covering the base and a present for Gracie May wrapped up ready for Christmas morning. The kitchen was as cold as the Russian Steppe, a stair separated it from the lounge and the frigid air settled into this lower area so that I could see my breath puffing out in front of me.

In the days after Christmas the snow eventually melted and
Gracie May and I looked out across houses lower in the valley as
the smoke from chimneys drifted upward and mingled with the
mists rising from Litton Woods. I let her out one morning when
the pale grass showed through the wind-ribbed remains of snow.
She stayed in the garden, sniffing, visiting every corner, jumping
on the fence and looking over into the field. Day by day she grew
bolder, until later in the winter I would see her way down the
field, drifting through the undergrowth like smoke, searching for
mice or sniffing at dead grasses and leaves. She would always
come home before dark and I was so glad of her company.

During this time, I felt alone and yet not lonely. The house was
friendly and welcoming; the neighbours on either side popped in
to say hello, my family and friends were only a few miles away
in Whitby. I was comforted to be so close to everyone I knew
and felt that my new home, though neglected, was a sanctuary. I
welcomed in 2004 with my parents and my sister Beth. My other
sister Clare, who lived in Edinburgh was enjoying the street acts
and fireworks of a traditional Edinburgh Hogmanay on Princes
Street. We called her to wish her Happy New Year.

'You should be up here with me!' she shouted down the line,
deafened by the sound of rockets exploding above the Royal
Mile.

'You should be down here with us!' we shouted back, happy that
she was enjoying herself among the colour and sound and
madness of the Scottish New Year. We raised a toast and I had a

great sense that this year would be a good one. As it turned out it was certainly one to remember.

## Chapter 10

I travelled to Hull regularly that winter, first to secure a letting agent that was not shy of the Nancy Grove area of the city, and then to check that the agent was showing tenants around my house and not just taking the fee and sitting with their feet up. I had reports from neighbours that the agent failed to turn up for viewings more than once. Things did not go to plan. Several people had enquired about the house, but nobody had yet signed a tenancy. I was concerned about leaving the place empty through the poor weather as an empty house in an area like this was soon a target for vandals. I remembered Alison's horror stories and I knew how important it was to let it out quickly.

I had some difficulty finding a builder to do the work required to get the house to a standard for letting. The garage had a flat roof which was in need of repair and though I had redecorated, there were problems with rain coming through a window that wouldn't close firmly enough. I seriously wondered if I had bitten off more than I could chew.

I had more luck however with getting a builder to help me in the lovely village of Rilldale back at Cat's Cradle. My ex-husband Richard put me in touch with a man who had worked for people locally for many years.

'He's a really good guy,' said Richard. 'He won't rip you off.' Richard and I had parted on good terms and I knew he would never want anything bad to happen to me. He had visited the cottage and approved of it, liking to think of Gracie May and I sitting by our fire, or me playing my piano in the winter afternoons.

When Rob came to look at the job I warmed to his easy good humour; he was honest, direct and kind. We drove around the countryside looking for just the right wood for the lintel over the fire and the right stone for the new fireplace. He was a man on his own with two daughters of nineteen and twenty one who both lived with him. He ran a house, a business and juggled a small number of loyal clients to give his girls the best life he could.

He shook his head at the patio doors which were almost falling out of their runners and ordered new ones that could withstand the blast of winter weather. He built a new staircase and repaired the roof, built steps to the kitchen door and a shed for the garden. The open fire looked good, but Rob told me it was dangerous. The bricks were not fire proof and could easily have exploded! He installed a wood burning stove where the open fire had been. When we lit the new Morso 'Squirrel' every room in the house became suddenly warm, including the chilly kitchen.

Rob had recently returned from a trip to Peru and I asked him to show me his photographs. He was surprised at my interest. 'No-one cares about a lonely man's travels,' he said, but he brought the photographs anyway. They marked him out as a true artist. There was the stark and abstract beauty of rock formations, the wonder of Machu Pichu, the sun reflected in an old man's eye and children's faces open with curiosity. I also noticed that when he approached a job he did it with the eye not of a jobbing builder, but of a master craftsman. The wood had to be just right, the finish perfect. I was surprised at the time and care he would take - every job he completed was a work of art.

During that spring we talked about everything; our interests, our lives, our loves, our heartaches. He talked about his border collie Bess, a feisty character with a passionate loyalty to her master. I was unaware of it at the time but he put me to the 'Bess test' the first day he invited me back to his home. He opened the door and Bess came rushing forward to greet him, but who was this strange woman? I held out my hand palm upwards and Bess sniffed at my fingers, then she let me pat her head, but she was wary and walked away with her tail tucked closely in. All through lunch she threw questioning glances in my direction. I didn't try too hard, but let her come to me in her own time. Bess came sniffing at me again, so I patted her and her tail wagged for just a second or two, a sign of a friendship beginning.

At Rob's house the shadowy flight of birds cut across the early spring sunshine streaming in at the windows. Pigeons soared upwards, hung on warm air currents and fluttered down to land on the roof of the loft in the garden. Rob used to race them, but now he just liked to have them around. His love of them went back to his days as a boy in 1966 when he had been a keen fan of the children's TV programme Blue Peter. He had entered a competition to decide on a pet for the show and his suggestion of a parrot, had won. Biddy Baxter invited him to travel down to the Shepherds Bush studios with his mother, an amazing trip to

London and one he and his mother had never made before. He met Valerie Singleton, Christopher Trace and John Noakes, (who was just about to join the show), and attended a party in the studio for all the children who had won prizes. The trip was the most exciting time of his young life, but every aspect of it paled into insignificance next to the wonder of *the prize*. This was better than any trip, better than the journey by train from York into Kings Cross, better even than meeting Patch the dog.

What was this glittering prize?

It was a book called Pigeon City.

Rob brought the book for me to see; a battered hard back. He had read it and reread it from cover to cover as a boy and again as an adult, enthralled at the idea of training birds to race the skies. The flight of birds became the expression of this young explorer's heart. The birds' freedom to wing their way from Cornwall or France was the freedom he wanted for himself. At the age of eleven he had bought his first pigeons and taught himself to care for them from his prize book. His enthusiasm hadn't dimmed and the day I first visited his home I got to meet birds that were direct descendants of that first precious purchase. I pictured a little boy, earnestly pressing his hard earned paper round money into the breeder's hand, his studious spectacles polished and his hair neatly combed. The local paper had run an article which covered both Rob's trip and that of a friend who had also won a prize. The photograph was captioned 'Two bright boys.'

While Rob worked on the house we ate lunch together at Cat's Cradle and sometimes he brought Bess with him. Before long she would happily play with me and would initiate our games by running up and down the room looking over her shoulder at me as if to say, 'Chase me!'

One early morning I lay in bed, contemplating the jobs that were still to do around the house. The wind was blowing hard and I could hear it buffeting at the windows and whistling down the chimney. Suddenly I heard something slide on the roof then breaking glass, immediately after that came a huge crash followed by a noise like fireworks which I later discovered was slate fragments falling from the roof and shattering on the concrete yard. I leapt out of bed and looked down on an extraordinary sight. The chimney pot was in the middle of the lawn, resting in a crater of its own making. I hastily pulled on some clothes and ran outside. The yard was covered with pieces of slate, the guttering was hanging off the roof like the leg of a crane fly and there was a hole in next door's pantry window. When I looked up, the chimney stack was leaning at a steep angle and looked ready to come down at any time. I realised I was in danger, if the stack didn't come down there could be debris which had yet to be dislodged. I went back inside and called Rob, praying that he hadn't left home yet for work. As soon as he answered the phone I burst into tears.

'Take your time and tell me the trouble,' he said and I babbled about the stack and the broken glass and the tiles.

'I'll come over now, don't worry, but while I'm getting to you there's an important job for you to do. You might need a pen and a piece of paper,' he said. I got out a tissue, blew my nose and went for a pen.

'I'm ready,' I said.

'Are you listening carefully? Ok write this down. Go to the shop and buy some Border Chocolate Gingers. Make sure they're Border Chocolate Gingers and not any cheap rubbish. Then come home, put the kettle on, put two Yorkshire tea bags into the pot and get two mugs out. You got that? Oh and make sure you have full cream milk, none of that watery semi- skimmed muck.'

When he arrived Rob surveyed the damage. He looked up at the stack which he judged was not in imminent danger of following the pot into the garden and we began to clear up.

'What am I going to do about it all?' I said later, a feeling of panic seizing me all over again. I wondered if my depleted budget could stand the thousands I expected it would take to put all this right.

'Not to worry,' said Rob. 'Just remember, miracles I can do straight away. The impossible takes only a little longer.'

Rob was true to his word. He sorted out next door's window, repaired the tiles and while some scaffolding was up for the roof next door, we arranged for the stack to be replaced. When the bill came it was well within my meagre budget. I felt I was on a ship with the best mate you could ever wish for. My mother had once advised me to join a club where I might meet someone to share my life, 'because no man is going to come knocking on your door.' But that's exactly what had happened with Rob. Within a couple of months we were inseparable. What had begun as a shared love of a pretty old house slowly developed over the following months into a love for each other.

'What would you have done if she hadn't taken to me?' I asked much later about his dog, Bess.

'I'd have known you weren't right for me and that would've been that,' said Rob. 'She can pick out a good heart better than I can.'

So you see I owe an awful lot to a black and white border collie called Bess.

## Chapter 11

The situation at Nancy Grove had not improved. I hadn't found any Hull builder who would take on the work, the letting agent seemed to be doing next to nothing about getting me a tenant and I was beginning to feel the financial pinch of paying for three mortgages, only one of which was covered by the income from rent. I was at least lucky that the tenants at Dellon Street continued to pay on time, and seemed content to remain where they were.

I explained my plight to Rob and he bravely accepted the challenge to leave Whitby and travel the two hours to Hull to look at the small house down a narrow street.

How I wished that Alison would take an interest in managing Nancy Grove for me but she wouldn't do it. 'It's on the wrong side of the tracks' she said. 'You should have listened when I told you.' Literally the house *was* on the wrong side of the tracks, there was a railway line between Dellon Street and Nancy Grove and though there were only four streets between them, I had a sense of discomfort when I turned into this part of Hull that I didn't have in Dellon Street. Alison was right. The new agency I had chosen was part of a big chain and they were not particularly reliable. More often than not they arranged viewings and didn't show up. My Nancy Grove neighbours told me a young couple had waited an hour to view the house before going off disappointed.

Eventually I gained a prospective tenant on my own, a Mr Howard, who had contacted me through a colleague at work and it was important to get the place right before he moved in. Rob began work on the house immediately and completed all the necessary work within a few short weeks. He suggested extra work which would make the house more attractive to potential tenants. This included a small kitchen extension and replacing the flat roof. I repapered and painted everywhere. By the time we had finished the place looked fit for a king. The tenant came to look around and was pleased with what we'd done. He was a single man who had a spaniel called Rex. We agreed that he would move in at the beginning of May, though I kept the agency on just in case things fell through.

At 5.30pm on April 24 I had a telephone message from the letting agent. The message was from a man called Nick.

'We've had a major problem with your house,' Nick said 'There has been some vandalism, but we have secured the building. You probably need to come and have a look tomorrow if you can.'

Shocked by the call I tried phoning him back but it was too late in the evening.

I called the police. I waited on the phone for forty minutes before I got through to a bored sounding officer. My heart pounded in my throat. What was the extent of the damage? What had been secured? Should we drop everything and go straight over there tonight? The police officer had few details. Something about the wall to the field, some damage to the property at the back, a conversation with the agent, but not to worry, the place was secure. An officer had seen it. Yes tomorrow would be soon enough.

I felt somewhat reassured after this conversation, but I don't think I slept more than a cat nap all night.

We called the agent early next morning.

'Vandals have demolished the wall to the field near your house and have damaged your back wall. We've boarded it all up so it is secure. Sorry, no, we have no one available to meet you there.'

Rob's van was out of action in the garage. The agent had secured the building but we still needed to find out what repairs were needed before Mr Howard and Rex could move in. We set off in my car.

We arrived in the middle of the morning. First, I walked along the street between the backs of the houses. I had made my way down the length of this street the week before, my hands clad in oversized thick rubber gloves picking up discarded carrier bags, old cans, broken bottles and disposable nappies and putting them into a skip I had hired for the building waste. I noticed that the street was still relatively clean. The wall at the end of the street however had been completely demolished. Standing five foot high, I wondered how anyone could have destroyed such a sturdy construction. There was a huge pile of rubble which spilled into the old burial ground and I could step across it to access the back wall of my house.

I took a step forward.

Looked.

Walked round to view it square on.

My spine turned to water and my knees gave way. Where the back wall of my house had been was a huge gaping hole. A flimsy board covered the door, but anyone who wanted to gain access could walk in though the open wall at the side. Someone had ripped out the newly fitted toilet and a great jet of water shot ten feet into the air, as though the life blood of the house were pumping away. I sat down hard on the pile of rubble. The wall at the end of the street had been attached to the rear wall of my house. We could see that people, (and quite a number would have been needed to do this), had rocked the wall until it collapsed, taking out most of the back wall of the converted garage.

Rob was by my side. Neither of us said a word for a few seconds -- which felt like minutes. My mouth was suddenly dry.

'Nice water feature,' said Rob and sat down beside me, taking hold of my hand. I became aware that there were other people nearby. Some older kids piling bits of wood and an old bicycle against an old oak tree had stopped to look at us. A woman with a child walked past and used the broken wall as a shortcut onto the back street.

'Aren't they wicked what done this?' she said calmly and walked past us over the stones, up the street I had cleared only last week. A lifetime ago.

'Will the house fall down?' I could hear my voice cracking. I had never been so glad of company.

'First thing we need to do is get someone to secure this and turn the water off,' Rob said, avoiding the question.

One of the kids approached us with mild interest. Confident. He wore a blue tee-shirt and grey sagging track suit bottoms. His face was pudgy and pale, with a couple of angry spots on his cheek.

'You need any help mate?' he said. Though the words were helpful, they felt like a threat. There was a barely concealed pleasure in the way he spoke; after all, he was a spectator at someone other person's misfortune. Someone he didn't know.

Other kids started to gather round.

'Who did it mate? What you gonna do?' They were in all probability the ones who had demolished the wall in the first place.

Rob was relaxed with them, and stood chatting while I walked round to the front door, let myself in, pulled out the phone directory and tried to find the numbers for an emergency plumber and a builder who would have the gear to make the wall safe. Without Rob's van, there was little he could do. Rob stayed where he was. If he left the back of the property unguarded we knew the kids would soon be inside, then we would have to call the police and it could all get ugly.

My fingers stumbled through the pages and I wanted to cry but I knew I had to get this done. I kept at it, willing myself not to break down. I could feel a draft from the hole in the wall as I made the calls. I found an emergency plumber and a firm of builders under A in the directory - Apollo construction. This sounded like an army of mythic warriors. When I had made the calls I sat by the phone feeling stunned. All we could do was wait.

After about half an hour a plumber arrived who looked like Sergeant Bilko from the old comedy show. He climbed out of his car with a hand towel draped over his arm, a torch and a small black box of tools. He wore a suit and tie and stood unhelpfully looking at the jet of water in dumb amazement. The stop- cock was somewhere in the street. Sergeant Bilko couldn't find it. Mr Apollo arrived shortly afterwards and turned out not to be an army of mythic warriors after all but a man on his own with a van. He couldn't find the stop cock either and nor could the five or so lads who had taken it upon themselves to 'assist'. One youth was using the water spout as a shower and began to whoop and dance around the jet like a Red Indian.

The odd thing was that nobody had been inside the house. The water was like an arrow pointing to a new and exciting place to explore but miraculously it seemed that nobody had taken much notice. There was even my set of step ladders with the rubber foot missing and a table and chairs all standing in full view of anyone who walked past, all untouched.

Sergeant Bilko had a cluster of youths around him. He wore heavy framed glasses which he kept pushing back up the bridge of his nose. One of the youths took hold of the small towel and twirled it out of his grasp. Bilko said 'Give me back my towel,' in a peevish high pitched voice. A part of me wanted to snigger. He was about as much use as a chocolate tea pot. Rob set about hitting the end of the water pipe with a hammer he had borrowed from Mr Apollo. Eventually the jet of water reduced to a drip, then with a deft hand Rob folded over the end of the pipe and hit it again until it was sealed. He and Mr Apollo measured the wall for boarding. Bilko told us there was nothing more he could do, would I please pay him the £80 call out fee and he would be on his way. He had done exactly nothing to help.

The two builders spent the afternoon making the wall to the garage safe with huge sheets of boarding. We piled the stones and bricks up against the bottom of the board to deter the youths from pulling at it.

'They still might fire it,' said Mr Apollo in a matter of fact way, motioning over to our audience with his head. 'But if I can get started on it tomorrow there's a chance that you won't lose your house.'

I felt cold. Rob put an arm around my shoulders. 'We'll stay here tonight and keep watch,' he said 'nobody will get in while we're here.'

That night was one of the worst of my life. Rob and I stayed in the house drinking coffee. There were no beds or blankets but that didn't matter, neither of us expected to get much sleep. As evening drew in we made periodic circuits around the house. The youths disappeared for a while and then came back. They were piling more wood against the oak tree.

'I hope you aren't thinking of doing anything stupid.' Rob said to one of the bigger lads, a thin, swollen eyed youth of about fourteen who was performing wheelies on a push bike far too small for him. A smaller boy stood miserably by the tree waiting. The larger youth didn't trouble himself to answer Rob, but cycled close to where he stood and spat within a couple of feet of his shoes. I had the feeling we were in a concrete forest with the wolves circling closer. Rob stood his ground and stared the youth down who cycled off, skidding the tyres on the worn turf.

Later we left the house again and I detected a distinct smell. Usually this was a smell that I loved, it reminded me of nights by the stove, bonfires, camping.

Woodsmoke.

We rushed around the side of the house to see flames reaching high into the branches of the oak tree, singeing the leaves and blackening the trunk. There were four of the original tribe staring up into the sparks, drinking from bottles of cider.

'Phone the police' said Rob.

The police came within ten minutes. As the flashing light appeared at the end of the street the youths melted away into the darkness. Two police officers, a dark haired young man and a pretty woman with blond hair and blue eyes came to help. Once we had pulled the fire apart, suffocated the flames with old towels and stamped on the embers they sympathised with us over a cup of tea. My eyes were stiff and sore from tiredness and worry.

'There isn't much we can do,' said Officer Noble, the dark haired man. 'As soon as we go they could come back. They've fired a couple of empty house up Woodcock Street and they've got a taste for it. If you take my advice, get the repairs done as soon as you can and get a tenant in here like yesterday. Otherwise I'm sorry to say you might lose your house.'

He was the second person to say this in one day; and they had both uttered these terrifying words as if people had their houses burned down every day.

'Nobody is going to burn this house down,' said Rob with the voice of reason. 'We won't leave it until it's secure.'

The youths did not come back that night. Though this didn't help us get any sleep. We spent the night playing with an ancient set of cards we found in a bedroom and drinking strong coffee. Mr Apollo turned up at eight am the next morning and we paid him to guard the site and prepare it for Rob to work on. While he did this, Rob and I returned to Rilldale to get the van and the materials he needed to build at double quick time.

I will always be grateful to Mr Apollo. He was a rough talking Hull man who could be foul- mouthed when the youths swore and threatened him, but he had a knack of getting them on his side too, and he even persuaded some of them to help move the rubble so that Rob could begin work. Mostly they were bored kids who jumped at the chance of being where the action was. I still think well of him, even when I saw him a couple of weeks later on Hessle Road, lifting a set of step ladders off his van; ladders with a missing rubber foot, the same set that strangely had gone missing from Nancy Grove.

'Nice ladders' I said

'Yeah ta,' he answered, and didn't blink an eye.

## Chapter 12

Mr Howard and Rex never did move into Nancy Grove. The work on the house took too long. I imagine they found a nice bungalow on the new estate near the park, and to be honest, it was a better place for them. When Rob had repaired the house I let it to Kelly, a single mum with a pierced tongue and a three year old called Lee. Occasionally I would drive over to Hull to see how things were going with Kelly and Lee. They were almost always asleep or out. Needless to say I had sacked the letting agent after our ordeal and was managing everything myself. Their misinformation had lost us sleep and had almost cost us the house.

On my visits the neighbours would come out and gossip with me on their front doorsteps. Pat and Kathy were two older women, both heavy smokers. Pat took a pride in her appearance and spoke of her plans to move into a house 'down the new park development'. Kathy's hair always looked as though she had just got out of bed. She came out with it pressed flat on one side with wayward tufts sticking out over her ears. Her thin clothes were frayed at the hem and cuffs and she told us she smoked fifty a day. Her voice was a chain saw, her laugh a cackle. One day Pat and Kathy told me there had been trouble, men coming and going from my house, sometimes more than one man in the house at a time, with shouting and the sound of things thrown about.

'She's not respectable' said Pat, fingering her fake pearls, her nostrils slightly flared. 'She's bringing the street down.' She leant forward into this last word and hissed in a low voice. How the street could be any lower than it already was I didn't know. They urged me to knock on the door, ask her how many men were in there today. That wasn't the only thing. A man wanted by the police had been living at number three. The police had come for him and he'd jumped through the window. Only thing was he didn't have time to open it first. I looked across at the pile of glass on the front yard and the dirty curtain flapping in the breeze.

'Dead' Kathy growled.

'What do you mean dead?'

'Killed hisself,' she said.

'On the glass.'

'Dear God.'

After that I decided I couldn't bear to manage the house myself. I found a new agent, waited each month for them to send the rent money and didn't visit the house again for a very long time.

## Chapter 13

By 2006 I had settled well into my new life in Rilldale. Rob and I had fallen into a pattern which suited us both of spending part of each week in each other's houses. That way we got to spend time with his girls, Rachel and Sarah, who were now both in their twenties and thinking of moving into flats of their own and also to spend time in our 'country home' doing the work which was still needed to get Cat's Cradle the way we wanted it.

Rilldale wasn't on the obvious tourist trail and there were very few holiday cottages in the village. Most of the houses were lived in all year round and this gave the place a vibrant, bustling feel. The school was thriving with plenty of new children coming up to join the infants. I found that people were community minded and thought nothing of arranging a working party to clean up an overgrown trod or to tidy up the tennis court. Nearby was the steam railway at Grosmont, pleasure boats at Ruswarp, and an Educational Moors centre at Danby and with Whitby only a few miles away there was always something new and interesting to do.

Rilldale had a fledgling theatre company, started up by two dynamic and well known theatre enthusiasts recently moved to the village. In Rilldale itself we had the railway station, three pubs, an excellent village shop and the famous Forden's butchers which people visited from miles around. Alfred Wainwright's Coast to Coast walk route came through the village and we often saw people trudging wearily past the house, asking how far it was to their lodging for the night, the Litton Arms. I remember 2006 as a year of warm sunny weather, but whenever I think of the walkers it is with rain dripping from their waterproofs and running down their faces, their shorts exposing cold mottled legs. They would have an expression of incredulity and dismay when I told them that although they were in Rilldale it was another mile of trudging until they reached their destination.

Rilldale had a tradition of opening its gardens to the public every year in a glorious display of summer flowers. Gardens ranged from diminutive spaces filled with a riot of pot plants to grand lawns and borders bursting with lupins, delphiniums, fiery red hot pokers and gladioli. There were ponds, water features, rockeries, romantic archways, garden rooms and conservatories dispensing home -made lemonade and ice cream. The church rooms were filled with crafts for sale and the village was flooded with people walking from garden to garden, stopping off for tea at the beautifully crafted village hall, The Robinson Institute.

A great draw during this open weekend were the amazing scarecrows, which people created either individually or in workshops organised to help make the best possible show. During a few days in June the village was transformed into a home for tennis stars, celebrities from film and TV, characters from nursery rhymes and fables. This year, elaborate scarecrows of a horse rider clearing a hedge, the entire cast of The Wizard of Oz including Toto, a coven of witches and many more decorated the grass verges on the road through the village. People arrived on bus trips to photograph the works of art. For us, the people who lived in the village, it was a time of excitement, bustle and activity -- all on our doorstep.

Rob and I took the weekend off to make the satisfying walk around the displays in the village and outlying farms. A great part of the pleasure was in meeting up with the new neighbours we only usually caught a quick word with in the shop. During open gardens we could drift around with friends or meet up with each other by a pond or a flower bed and catch up on the past year. Rob and I hadn't managed to make scarecrows of our own, but we admired the work of others. My garden was still very much a work in progress, and I gained inspiration from the other small patches of ground people had transformed into pocket sized explosions of colour.

A number of small holdings took the opportunity to sell vegetables, bread, eggs and other produce. We paid two pounds for a dozen free range eggs of various sizes, which we found at the end of a neighbour's track. When we peeped inside the boxes the eggs were clearly from different hens; some were small, thin-shelled and pale which rattled in their cardboard chambers like fragile marbles, some were speckled brown, promising deep yellow yolks and some were a delicate duck egg blue, a much more interesting collection than the drab perfection of supermarket fare. We also collected a few stalks of rhubarb, a pot of marmalade and a fruit cake as we walked around. The sun filtered through the early green of oaks and ash, and we sat in the shade of a hornbeam to take in the view and chat with Rita and Mike who owned a smallholding. They kept hens, ducks, ponies, sheep, goats and another more interesting addition to the valley – Llamas. These stepped around their field surveying their territory with long lashed grace, gazing down on us mere mortals from the regal vantage point of their higher ground.

A dark cloud had scattered a few fat raindrops over the gardens, but it had soon blown over. Now as we four stood and looked on with glasses of wine in our hands, we saw the white clouds part, and low sunlight lay a trail of gold across the ripening fields and shine on wisps of fleece caught on wire. It made me think of Virginia Woolf's The Waves. '*The day waves yellow with all its crops.*'

That evening I opened a box to use a couple of eggs in a cake, and found three of them had disappeared. Rob said he didn't know what had happened to them and it seemed a complete mystery to me that one moment they were there and the next they were gone.

Chapter 14

If it seemed that my Hull worries were at an end that wasn't quite true. The situation at Nancy Grove cast a shadow over my happiness. I was becoming weary and fearful of the phone calls from Pat and Kathy, the agent calling to tell me that the gas fire had been condemned, that Kelly's 'boyfriend' had smashed a window or that Kelly was complaining that the third bedroom access was dangerous because it only had a step ladder. (There was no third bedroom, the step ladder led to the loft).

One spring day I had a call from Kathy to say she thought Kelly was no longer living at the house. I called Kelly on her mobile. She was living with her mother further up Hessle road. 'They've all got it in for me down there. Keep calling me names. I'm not going back.'

Rob and I opened the door to Nancy Grove on a warm day. It was the first time I had returned to Hull in a year. The smell was awful. Food was left out on the kitchen surface; a jug of what had been milk, a green loaf of bread and a half empty can of beans were on the kitchen table. An old packet of basic brand cat biscuits was scattered across the floor. Mould covered the interior of the unplugged fridge and a load of clothes was still immersed in the washing machine. In the lounge, toys were strewn around the carpet and a pair of tights straddled the back of the sofa. Three photographs of Kelly and Lee in a McDonald's restaurant hung in lopsided frames above the fire. Upstairs the wardrobes were full of clothes. More toys and cheap cosmetics cluttered the bathroom. None of this prepared me for what I saw in the back yard. Here Kelly had piled up around thirty black bin liners full of rubbish; ordinary domestic waste that hadn't been taken out for refuse collection. In the warm sunshine, the smell of rotting food was nauseating.

'Cafe, coffee, rubber gloves and cleaner,' said Rob and I nodded silently. What else was there to say?

I texted Kelly about the contents of the house though I thought it hopeless to ask her about the rubbish.

'Get rid of it,' was the curt reply. I guessed that was her way of giving notice.

I sent another message about returning the key, but she didn't respond.

After fortifying ourselves with strong mugs of coffee in the local cafe, we set about sorting out the house. We had walked into a snapshot of Kelly's last day in the house, and it was as though someone had told her a bomb was about to drop and she had to leave everything immediately. I had come across such sad scenes occasionally when I had been house hunting, but these were usually the result of the bailiffs ejecting people who had defaulted on a mortgage once too often.

What had been the last straw that had finally made Kelly turn the lock on all her clothes, photographs, Lee's toys and leave? Had her failure to take out the rubbish simply been due to an inability to get out of bed? What kind of life was that?

It took us three days to clear the house. We arranged for a private refuse collection and also took Kelly's old life, the belongings she had left behind, in bag after bag to the tip. I felt bad for her and Lee. I imagined her eventually getting another house in some other shabby corner of town, housing benefit paying her rent, a period of calm before the neighbours noticed the callers, put two and two together - and turned their backs once again.

The area of Hull around Nancy Grove felt dangerous and lawless. The two hour drive could as easily be taking me to another country where none of the rules I had come to expect applied.

When we left the house it was clean and fresh. On the way home I instructed an agent to put it on the market.

## Chapter 15

The summer weather was stifling. The beginning of July came in burning like a brand and visitors to Whitby walked around with arms and faces scorched from over exposure to the sun. A heat haze lay on the sea's horizon and boats bobbed lazily out of the harbour bulging with people desperate for a breath of cool salt air. Out on the moors skylarks sang wildly as they flickered in the blue air. Unshorn sheep panted under the weight of their fleeces and trailed the peeling wool in clumps behind them.

Rob's pigeons lay listlessly in the loft, or sat on its roof raising one wing at a time as he played a thin spray of water towards them to cool them off. The heat was the subject of conversation in the shops and between people when they met in the street.

'Hot enough for you?' said old farmers to each other, each wearing a thick shirt, braces, corduroy trousers and a lined cap.

'As hot as the summer of 76,' said many.

On the morning of July 17 I was setting the table ready for breakfast at Rob's house. He had put the coffee on to percolate and we were having wholemeal toast and blackcurrant jam. I remember the details because what came next was such a surprise.

I heard the sound of Rob's boots scraping hurriedly up the garden path. It was a sweltering morning and I went out of the back door to see what was making him move so fast in the heat.

He held something small in his hands and rushed past me to the back of the kitchen.

'Hold this,' he said and handed me a tiny bundle of skin and feather.

'That's not a pigeon squab.' I said stupidly looking down at a madly cheeping beak on legs. I noticed a blood stain between its wing stumps near the back of its neck.

'No, it's a hen chick,' said Rob and brought out some chick crumbs from a box in his pantry.

'How can it be a hen chick?' I said, handing it back to him.

Rob had a damp piece of cotton wool in his hand and was gently dabbing at the chick's wound which thankfully looked fairly superficial.

'Because it hatched out of a hens egg that's how', said Rob and smiled.

'I don't understand.'

'Remember the eggs we bought from Rita and Mike?' he said.

'Yes,' I said, still not understanding.

'Well I took three of them and put them under the pigeons.'

'What?'

The eggs had been free range. Rob had reckoned they might be fertilised and had decided to see if he could hatch some out. He didn't have an incubator, and thought of his pigeons.

'But the eggs were in a box, they were cold,' I said.

'The eggs stay dormant until they have the right conditions and then they start to develop,' said Rob.

I was amazed. I hadn't known it was possible to take fertilised eggs and incubate them like this. As it turned out neither had Rob, but he thought it was worth the experiment and it worked. The only thing that concerned him was that hens sit on their eggs for three days longer than pigeons. He had left three eggs in the loft; one of his broody pigeons had claimed them as her own and had been faithful to them for 21 days. After this, she abandoned them. Undeterred, Rob had placed them in the warmest part of the loft and the hot weather had done the rest. Only one of the eggs had made it to maturity, but here was the evidence before my eyes, a tiny, ugly, hot bag of bones with very strong lungs. The pigeons, quick to recognise this was a bit of a cuckoo in their nest had attacked and injured her and would have succeeded in killing her if Rob hadn't come to the rescue.

'What on earth are we going to do with her?' I said, watching her peck at the chick crumbs with enthusiasm.

'Keep her of course,' said Rob. 'Or him.'

That's all we needed, a lone cockerel strutting about the garden.

## Chapter 16

'We are trying very hard to sell your house Mrs Ritson,' said the agent, a young woman with a clipped voice.

'But the fleas are putting people off,'

'Fleas? But there haven't been any animals in the house.' I said, as the memory of that box of cat biscuits scattered across the floor flashed across my mind.

'Well there are fleas,' replied the clipped voice with barely disguised disgust.

'We'll come over,' was all I could say. Absurdly I felt guilty, as though we had bred the fleas ourselves, but we had left the house clean and most definitely flea free. What had happened to it since we were last there?

Before Rob and I could arrange our visit, I had a call from fifty-a- day Kathy.

'You got a downstairs window open love,' she rasped 'They'll be in there doing mischief if you don't come.'

How I wished I had left a key with her, she could have let herself in and shut the window for me. Why hadn't I? The fact was I didn't trust her. She considered jumping through a window and dying on the concrete below as routine an act as going out for a packet of cigs. Kathy had laughed to me about shop lifting from the nearby Asda and confided that her son visited her on benefit day to steal her money. A key given to her might easily go astray. The thief would use the house as a squat, fire it or smash it up. The best thing was to get over there as soon as possible, sort out the pests and the open window at the same time, get someone interested in the house and move it on.

We'd had a quote from a local pest control firm and they told us they would charge £200 to treat the house.

What would they do for that I asked?

Spray it with flea spray.

I didn't have £200.

Rob and I bought three industrial sized cans of flea spray, put wellingtons in the boot of the car and set off. We would have to drive there and back in one day because I had a work meeting I couldn't reschedule the next day.

Before we walked up to the house we put on our wellingtons and tucked our jeans into the tops. We didn't want any biting pests getting at our ankles. The sun beat down from a clear sky and when I put my hand on the roof of the car to steady myself as I pulled on a boot, the metal burned my fingers. I saw the open downstairs window as soon as we turned into the Grove. The gap was a good five inches wide, it was an easy target for anyone who wanted to get inside. I was surprised that nobody had done it already.

'How long's it been like that?' I asked Kathy, who had dragged herself out of the house in torn slippers.

'Few days, didn't see anyone go in though,' she wheezed, holding onto the fence, breathing hard in the heat.

'Going on a moon walk?' she said, glancing at our footwear, her rasp of laughter like a death rattle.

We let ourselves in. There was no doubt about it; somebody had been in since we were last there. A plastic carrier bag was on the sofa and a plate was on the kitchen floor. Otherwise everything seemed the same as when we had left it, apart from the fleas. The estate agent had been right about those.

'Kelly must've been back in, maybe under cover of darkness, she's the only one who has a key that we know of,' said Rob.

'But why would she do that?'

He shrugged.

'We'll get this done then I'll change the lock,' he said.

Being a part time pest control operative was not high on my list of favourite jobs. The heat was like a sauna and we left the window open while we worked, but still we were gasping for breath as we finished each room. Upstairs I entered the back bedroom and saw a pile of newspaper that hadn't been there before. I left it and sprayed the front bedroom first, and then I went up into the loft which brought me out in fresh pinpricks of sweat. I didn't want to undo all our good work by failing to do the job thoroughly.

When I went into the bedroom again I thought I saw the newspaper flutter, though that was impossible because there was no draft and the window was closed. I walked over to the far end of the room to investigate.

I looked down.

The newspaper moved again and I saw a tiny pink paw.

I looked closer and one of a litter of five tiny kittens lifted its head and scrabbled confusedly, mewling quietly.

**'Kittens! There are kittens!'** I squealed.

'What did you say?' Rob shouted and soon we were both looking down at a wriggling ball of fur and whiskers in a nest of crumpled up old newspaper.

'The open window!' I said

'For the mother to get in.' said Rob

'Dumped them here and hoped for the best,' I said.

'Look at them!' I said. And look at them we did; two black and white ones, a ginger and white one and two tabbies. We left the bedroom unsprayed so that the fumes didn't damage their immature lungs and waited.

And waited.

As time went on the kittens began to scrabble about more urgently. We left them and moved into a back room downstairs, so as not to frighten the mother if she returned. After three hours there was no sign. I was getting anxious that the kittens would need their next feed and I had no idea what we would do if she didn't turn up. What do you do with very tiny kittens if they don't have their mother's milk? I rang our local vet in Whitby for advice. The vet told us that if the mother didn't arrive soon they would become dehydrated and this could damage them very quickly; they could die if left for more than eight hours. The vet had kitten milk powder and feeding bottles, but they were due to close for the day. We couldn't leave the kittens and hope that the mother cat would return, because that meant leaving the house insecure with an open window. We couldn't stay, because I needed to get home and prepare for my meeting the next day. We had a two hour journey in front of us. If we brought the kittens home would the vet leave the feeding equipment out for us? Yes, he would leave it in a steel bin outside the door. We had to make a decision.

At eight o'clock in the evening Rob changed the lock to the house; we closed the window, found a shoe box in a cupboard, lifted the kittens into it and sprayed this last bedroom.

We saw Kathy on the way out and she peeped into the box.

'Got a bucket you can borrow if you want,' she said.

'We're taking them home,' I said. Kathy choked back a laugh and shook her head.

'Will you call us if you see the mother?' I asked

'If you like,' she said, but I knew she wouldn't.

The kittens calmed down and slept on the way home, it was as if they knew that the more they moved the weaker they would make themselves, and that we were doing our best to get them to safety.

It was getting dark by the time we pulled into the vet's car park. There was no sign of a steel bin. We got out of the car and looked around. If he had forgotten to leave the milk powder we were in trouble. A thin misty rain began to fall and the warm tarmac radiated humid warmth. The ginger and white kitten looked up when we opened the box lid, his bright unfocused eyes moved about in his overlarge head as if to say enough is enough, where's my dinner? He looked like a real bruiser already, his head was almost twice the size of his body which gave him an odd out of proportion look, he was grubby and I was sure I caught sight of a flea running across his scrawny belly.

We had no torch so we searched by the light of the street lamp which had just flickered into light. The smell of seaweed was strong tonight, brought in on drifts of air from the exposed beach. We could hear the muffled roar as the waves sucked in and out far down the sand.

There was no bin.

'Let's try round the back, there may be another door,' said Rob and we blundered round the side of the building which was deep in shadow.

I stumbled over a brick.

'If only we had a torch!' I said

'How could we have known that today we would find a litter of motherless kittens, bring them home in the dark and that we would need to find milk powder in the pitch black?' said Rob. He had a point.

At last we reached a side door, there was no sign of a bin, but as reached for the door handle to steady myself I felt that something was hooked over it. It was a carrier bag. I lifted it off the handle and brought it into the light. Inside were five tiny bottles, a carton of milk powder and a measuring scoop. I was so relieved I started to laugh.

Quickly we drove back home. As soon as the car stopped moving the kittens became restless, they reached out with their paws and moved their heads around curiously. The instructions told us to mix up the feed with boiled water and then leave it to cool to blood temperature, and to feed them what seemed a tiny amount each. I lifted out the ginger and white kitten first. He looked the strongest and most able to adapt to this strange new way of getting his food. Once the feed was ready I held him gently in

one hand, with a finger over the top of his head and my thumb
under his wobbling chin and moved the teat of the bottle close to
his enquiring mouth. At first he didn't seem to understand that
here was something good. It may not come from something
large, warm and furry, but it was the closest thing to having a
mother he was going to have from now on. I shook a couple of
drops onto his lips and he licked them hesitantly. Then he licked
the end of the teat and I squeezed it gently so that another couple
of drops fell out onto his pink tongue. He seemed to approve of
this because he suddenly latched onto the bottle and began to
suck at it, swallowing big hungry mouthfuls. His bright blue eyes
squeezed shut and he seemed in ecstasy as he drained the bottle
dry. Immediately he had finished drinking he was asleep, his
body relaxed and he let out a short wheezing sigh as his head
lolled backwards. We placed him in an old washing up bowl with
a cushion and a piece of blanket. So far so good. Rob tried with
one of the black and white kittens; this one had a slightly more
hesitant start but soon got the hang of it. Then we fed a kitten
each, until we came to number five.

We could see that the four kittens we had successfully fed so far
were males. This fifth kitten, one of the tabbies, was a female
and she was much smaller and thinner than the others. While
they had all been in the box together she was hidden under a pile
of fur, but once we had fed the others and placed them gently
into the washing up bowl we could see how fragile she was. She
had such a delicate and beautiful face, the tabby marking around
her cheek bones were symmetrical and dramatically dark around

her sea blue eyes, making her look Egyptian. We called her Tabitha. Tabitha was trying hard to open her jaw sufficiently wide around the teat of the bottle. Only after a few failed attempts did she manage it, but her ability to suck was not as strong as the others, and it took us a long time to get that first feed inside her. Before it was finished she had fallen asleep, the teat falling from her closed mouth and droplets of milk running down the sides of her face. The effort had exhausted her. I dabbed her clean with a damp piece of kitchen paper.

We now had five kittens snoozing and whistling softly in their sleep. Rob and I looked at each other like proud parents. It wasn't an ideal situation for the kittens to be without their mother, and it was certainly far from ideal for us to suddenly gain the responsibility of feeding five hungry mouths for the next few weeks, but we had made our decision back at Nancy Grove, and there was no going back on it now.

Before we turned in to bed we made up five new bottles of milk ready for the next feed, and placed the washing up bowl next to us in the bedroom. I set the alarm on my phone. At two am the alarm raised me from sleep and I saw that the kittens were scrambling around in their nest, awake and ready for food. I boiled the kettle and stood the bottles in the warm water until the temperature raised sufficiently. I tested the milk on the inside of my wrist and only when it felt blood temperature did I start to feed them. I began this time with Tabitha, I thought that the sooner she was fed the better chance she stood of surviving. Rob had also woken up by now and was feeding one of the black and white kittens. This one had a lovely blaze of white down his nose, which split into two flames curling upward towards his eyes, the other was covered in black blotches like ink blots, one of which covered an eye like a pirate's patch. We called these two Blaze and Blot.

Tabitha managed better at this feed and seemed to have understood she almost had to dislocate her poor little jaw to get hold of the teat. We helped her by squeezing the milk onto her tongue but it took a long time for her to empty the bottle. The others were feeding like old hands and we were soon laying them back in their nest, their tiny paws relaxing to reveal each individual soft pink pad.

The alarm woke us again at five am and we went through the whole process again, Tabitha first, then we alternated with the others so that none of them always had to wait until last. Ginger was drinking twice as much as the others; he was strong and sturdy and began to look for the teat as though that was all he had ever known.

Gracie May suffered our new guests with ill-concealed disgust. She didn't come near the basket and if I encouraged her closer she spun on her heel and flounced away. 'It's not for long,' I told her. 'We'll find homes for them and then it'll just be the three of us again'. One cat was definitely enough. We agreed to advertise them for good homes as soon as we had weaned them.

After the eight o'clock feed, feeling tired but pleased with our first night's efforts, we took the litter for the vet to check them over. Simon examined each tiny specimen of cat life separately. He picked them up, turned them around, looked in their eyes and ears, examined their rears, took their temperatures and declared them all healthy.

'The small female might struggle, but she would have been the weak one in the litter any way.'

'The runt?' I asked

'Yes, the mother may have rejected her in time, but this way she stands a reasonable chance of survival.'

He told us we would need to feed them every two hours for the next two weeks at least, then we could experiment with leaving them a little longer at night. He treated them for fleas with a puff of powder on the back of the neck and the base of the tail.

Apparently we would have to be a mother to them in every way.

'Mother cats lick their kitten's bottoms to make them pass faeces,' said Simon

'Well I draw the line at that!' I said

'You'll have to rub their bottoms gently with some damp cotton wool to stimulate them. They can't do it on their own, their mother's tongues are rough, so you will have to be fairly vigorous.'

Simon thought the kittens were about twelve days old, give or take a day. That meant they had been born on around 17 July, the same day that our chicken had hatched. When we returned home I circled the date on the calendar so that I could tell the new owners approximately how old their kittens were.

The next time we fed each kitten we took pieces of damp cotton wool and rubbed each bottom briskly. Ginger quickly got the hang of it and I was absurdly delighted by a show of yellowish inoffensive goo. Blaze and Blot also took to this new part of the routine well. The Tabby male, which we now called Tiber took a long time to respond. We rubbed and encouraged and he looked around at us in surprise but nothing happened. With Tabitha the story was much the same. She was so slight that I needed to be very gentle with her, and when I rubbed, her little back end wobbled from side to side. She closed her eyes as though concentrating her effort, but produced nothing.

When it came time for the evening feed, Tiber drank more than his usual share of the milk and, as though he had been thinking about what he needed to do next, he managed to mark the cotton wool. I was so pleased at our progress. This meant we only had to get Tabitha into the routine and we would have five healthy, correctly performing kittens. The problem was that Tabitha didn't seem able to respond as the others had. She would close her eyes, and straighten her tiny legs with the effort of trying, but nothing happened at all. The other thing was that she seemed very sleepy most of the time. When the others were clamouring for food, she was always the last one to get up out of the nest and the first to fall asleep after each feed. I knew that it couldn't be good to keep all that waste inside her so the next day I took her back to the vet.

Simon felt her haunches, and pressed gently around her bowel area. Tabitha sat calmly as though she knew she was in good hands.

'I think she has a blockage,' he said. She's so tiny it may be impossible for us to work on her successfully, but I'm willing to give it a go if you'd like to leave her.'

There was nothing to do but let Simon try his best.

Later that day I went back to find out what had happened.

'Well I've managed to create some movement,' said Simon

'She has passed a quantity of waste, but I am concerned it may be bypassing an impacted mass that has become hard and difficult to dislodge. I think we need to prepare ourselves for the fact she may not survive.'

He advised that I take her home and try the feeding and bottom rubbing routine at home again. Poor little Tabitha, she looked completely done in. At home, she swayed to her feet while the others moved keenly towards the source of food, and she fell asleep after only a small amount of food was inside her. She did pass waste a few times and I became cautiously confident that once her strength was built up she would gradually take more and more food.

We carried on like this for a few days. Tabitha would drink about a half bottle of milk before falling immediately to sleep. The others had begun to trample her underfoot as they grew in confidence.

Six days after the kittens came home I took Tabitha out of the washing up bowl and placed her in her own tiny box, lined with a piece of torn soft towel. She barely raised her head now when I approached with her feed and it seemed that I was disturbing her when I let milk droplets fall onto her mouth hoping that she would lick her lips. She seemed to have lost her ability to suck at the teat and she now slept almost all the time. She could still stand, but she staggered to her feet like a miniature drunk and sometimes fell over before I could gently pick her up. Even though it was summer time, she began to feel cool, so on the seventh night I half filled a rubber bottle with tepid water, placed the towel over it, and laid Tabitha on top of it. Her tiny jaw was set hard now, and she had squeezed her eyes closed. She breathed in tiny ragged snatches, sometimes seeming to stop, but then struggling to take one more breath. I got up for her every two hours during the night, refilled the bottle, testing it to make sure it was not too warm and I stroked her shrunken frame. At about four in the morning I took her out of the box and held her in the palm of my hand, at last I even sang a song to her. She stopped breathing at about twenty past four. Just one long outbreath and nothing more, like a sigh.

# Cat's Cradle

We wrapped her body in tissue and buried her in the garden rockery near a miniature poppy. I had only known that tiny kitten for a week, but I am not ashamed to say that I cried.

## Chapter 17

Meanwhile the boys were getting stronger. We had moved them into the bathroom because here we could keep them safely shut in and they had the freedom to roam around as they became stronger. We just had to be sure and keep the toilet lid closed. I didn't want any casualties getting lost down the bowl!

The other consideration was our new chick, which we were sure was a male and had christened George. We couldn't let George loose in the pigeon loft as this would have been a death sentence for him, and we couldn't keep him with us either. My bathroom seemed to Rob to be the perfect solution, 'Just until he gets a bit stronger. He thinks we are his parents,' he said. It was madness but I reasoned that the bathroom was already taken up with kittens, what difference would a chicken make? It was a rough and ready room, carpeted with an offcut and we hadn't yet got around to upgrading it to the bathroom of my dreams. George and the kittens could keep each other company. After all they were exactly the same age and were growing up together.

There were some logistical problems about ensuring the kittens were fed at the right time every day. I worked from home, but there were days when I needed to travel and was away from early morning until tea time. Rob had his building work and this took him anywhere within a ten mile radius of home each day. On the days when I was away from the house, we packed the kittens into their bigger box, the washing up bowl had soon become too small for them and Rob took them in the work van to whatever job he was busy with. He would ask if there was a room he could place the sleeping kittens in until their next feed. His customers were all so understanding and they were charmed at Rob, the surrogate dad, though he did raise a few eyebrows with some of his tougher clients. He stopped his building work periodically to wipe the stone dust and mud from his hands and face and heat up prepared bottles of feed in warm water, then he sat on a wall and fed his four furry charges in the middle of the site. After their feed they would go back to sleep and be no trouble at all until the next feed was due.

The ginger kitten outpaced his brothers and seemed to be getting larger by the hour. Blaze and Blot were coming along well and Tiber was increasing the amount he drank at every feed. After a couple of weeks we left them asleep at eleven pm and didn't feed them again until five am. This seemed to suit them and it was certainly far better for us.

Ginger was independent and tough. He would drink two full bottles of feed then watch us feed the others before dropping off to sleep again. He was bolder too, exploring the bathroom and facing up to George the chicken who was growing so quickly he soon towered over them. When George came near them the other kittens drew back unsure of what to make of him, but Ginger would raise a curious paw.

George considered Rob to be his parent. If anything frightened him he would run to Rob and stand on his foot, clucking in alarm. Rob could even walk around with the chicken balanced on the end of his toe. During this time Rob would get into the bath and George would hop on his chest and sit there quite happily while Rob worked at his crossword book. I wouldn't have believed it if I hadn't seen it with my own eyes. The place was beginning to feel like a menagerie and my only way of feeling sane during this time was to know that the end was in sight. Soon the kittens would be ready to rehome, George would be mature enough to return to the loft, and would have grown bigger than those pigeons that had pecked him when he first hatched.

When they were about four weeks old the kittens slept in a corner of the bathroom and only went in their box when we needed to take them with us. One kitten stood out from the others as the most affectionate. Little Blaze, his face marked with twin white flames was always the first to run towards me when I went into the bathroom to feed them. He would paw at my leg, mew loudly then after he had been fed he loved to crawl up my arm and fall asleep near my ear.

We took them to friends' houses whose children delighted in having a turn at feeding and loved to play with them as they scampered about, pouncing on pieces of paper and chasing string. As they became older and slept less we bought a small net play pen, just perfect for our four sturdy kittens.

Soon it was time to think about getting my kitten family new homes. I thought of advertising in the local paper, or on the noticeboard of the local shop but I hesitated at this became I felt very protective towards my little brood. My kittens were so used to humans they thought they *were* human. However, I knew that I couldn't keep all four of them and I had to think of something. Then I began to worry what if nobody wanted them? What if the new family didn't treat them properly? What if they gave them a life outdoors with little human contact? I couldn't bear the idea of any one of our hand reared kittens being treated like a farm cat.

My father was a keen botanist. He had retired early and spent many contented days roaming the fields and moors of the area identifying flowers, ferns and mosses. The Whitby Naturalists had approached him to run a workshop and a Whitby Gazette reporter had arranged to interview him about it.

'Why don't you get the Gazette to run an article on the kittens? That way people will hear the whole story and it might encourage those who really care about animals to come forward, he said.

It was a great idea.

When the kittens were nearly five weeks old I gave the Gazette a call. They told me it was just the sort of story they wanted and they would be happy to come along to interview me and photograph the kittens. On a warm dewy morning at the beginning of August, Sally from the Gazette turned up to interview me about how the kittens came to Cat's Cradle. As I told my story I realised it was quite a tale and I began to feel optimistic that kind new owners would come forward, people who would love and care for 'my boys'. I told Sally about Tabitha and how bravely she had fought to hang onto her life, but that she hadn't made it, and I told her about how our chicken, George, had come into the world and how the kittens shared the bathroom with him. Sally listened intently as I told the story of the hens eggs which Rob had placed under the pigeons.

'Could I write about your chicken too?' she said 'it's just the sort of quirky tale our readers are interested in.'

I hadn't really considered that the events of that summer would be of interest to anyone else but I agreed. Sally had brought a photographer with her and he took a photograph of George perched on Rob's shoulder. We took the kittens out into the back garden and the photographer positioned me in front of them crouched on the ground, while he lay on the grass ready to shoot, both of us getting drenched in the dew.

Rob took the kittens about ten feet away and let them go. It was the first time any of them had been outside for more than a moment and at first they just stood there completely still, frowning into the sun, looking minute and fragile in the open air, then they caught sight of me and began to scamper in my direction. Blaze as usual was out in front in his eagerness to reach me. Ginger was distracted by the grass and the flowers. Tiber and Blot both ran in my direction for a brief moment and then were surprised by a passing butterfly and looked away. The photographer however had caught that moment when they were first released and all facing in the same direction. It was their moment of fame.

We had thirty eight offers of new homes for the kittens following the article. It was an amazing response. A neighbour who only lived a couple of doors up the road from me in Rilldale rang to say she hadn't known about the kittens until now and could she take both Ginger and Blot, but would I mind if she changed Blot's name to Charlie? Of course I didn't mind at all. Blot wasn't a very dignified name after all and was only temporary, to help me identify him.

I knew I wouldn't be keeping him and the name I had given him somehow made it easier to let him go. I knew as they developed that the kitten's characters might suggest very different names from those I first gave them.

Another family came, looked at the two remaining kittens and chose Tiber. It wasn't difficult to see why. Tiber ran over to them straight away and was happy to let their little boy pick him up and cuddle him, whereas Blaze curled up into a ball and fell asleep.

'I think we'll keep the name you gave him,' they said 'It could be short for Tiberius and we can see he is as strong as a Roman Emperor.'

Another family was due to come and see Blaze but a strange and very sad thing happened which made me change my mind about letting him go and I called them to let them know I had already found a home for him. I just didn't let on that the home was with me.

Gracie May had reluctantly agreed to share her new home with the four kittens and George the hen. They were no trouble to her as they were almost always locked in the bathroom, asleep or being fed. I had never seen a cat frown before, but whenever she caught sight of any of them she would screw up her face and stalk off as though we had insulted her. She spent much of her days sitting in the garden by the fence, where I had planted roses as I had at Deyton. From this vantage point she could watch for mice scurrying out from the hedge, or insects coming in to land on the flowers. She would often keep me company as I hung out the washing, or dug in the borders.

Over the short weeks since the kittens had arrived she had put on a great deal of weight, and her belly seemed unnaturally swollen. I took her to the vet who could find nothing wrong. She didn't seem in pain, but sometimes when I went to stroke her she would hiss and look as though she wanted to scratch me though she never did. Then quite suddenly the extra weight seemed to melt away and she returned to her old size and character. It was curious, but I was so busy with other things that I didn't question what had happened too closely.

It was the end of August. The house was unnaturally quiet now that all but one of the kittens had gone to their new homes. While I had been busy with them the weeds in the garden at Cat's Cradle had grown quickly in the showery weather.

I went out one morning to weed between my new roses; a time consuming and prickly business. I had a number of David Auste Eglantyne bushes which were producing glorious light pink blooms with a scent of old rose. I had mingled these with the deep crimson and richly scented Munstead Wood with their rich cups of loose petals. At one end of the garden I had planted a fev blackcurrant bushes and raspberry canes. I had gathered the blackcurrants back at the end of July but the raspberry canes were still heavy with fruit. For some quick colour I had scattered nasturtiums and the last of the sweet peas clambered up sticks bound together into a frame. Gracie May sat by the fence and watched as I dug out the weeds on my hands and knees with my trowel. Every now and then I would stand up to stretch my legs and look out over the view I never tired of, across the field to the solitary oak and down to Litton woods with its gently drifting canopy of mist. I spent a good hour enjoying the feel of the earth under my hands and breathing in the scent of damp blossom. I spoke to Gracie May as I moved between the roses and she sat with her legs tucked under her like a contented hen, her eyes half closed in the sunshine. It was a time of companionship, rare after the days of frantic feeding.

I stopped my weeding and unrolled the hose to give my newly turned soil a good soaking. I began at one edge of the garden and slowly moved closer and closer to where Gracie was sitting. I was now so close that I thought it odd she hadn't moved. Usually she would have jumped out of the way of stray drops of water, but she sat on, her eyes half closed as though in a dream. I had a

92

feeling that she had been sitting there a very long time. Hadn't I looked out that morning and seen her in that same position, the one she often took up when she was looking for movement in the grass? I turned off the water and walked over the check on her. I reached out my hand and touched her soft grey head.

She was dead.

I couldn't take it in. She had seemed so contented sitting there but here she was, her pretty eyes unblinking, looking as though she were still enjoying the sun. I hurriedly cast my mind back to when I had been speaking to her, and remembered her turning her head as I moved past her spot and told her how beautiful she was. She had seemed fine then and that was, what, twenty minutes ago? There was no sign of pain or suffering of any kind and she hadn't moved at all from the position she had been calmly sitting in all morning. But now she was dead.

I lifted her out of the hedge and brought her into the house, her body limp and heavy. There were no marks anywhere on her body. What had happened was a complete mystery. I sat there for quite some time just stroking her and looking at her in disbelief. My lovely Gracie May who had braved the main road in Deyton, dodging between the traffic to greet me, had succumbed to death quietly by the hedge with no danger in sight.

I was heartbroken.

I called Rob to let him know what had happened and he came home early so we could bury her. He dug a hole in the garden

near the fence she had so loved to sit by. We lowered her into it
scattered a few rose petals over her pretty grey body, thanked he
for coming into our lives and said goodbye.

The next morning my eyes were still red and swollen from
crying.

# Cat's Cradle

## Chapter 18

Rob had been a builder most of his working life. After a short spell in a butcher's shop he completed a seven year apprenticeship to a builder. Once he had worked for a building company for a few years he left to set up on his own. It was a tough life. Compared with my physically undemanding work, which often presented a challenge of a different kind, Rob's days were marked by heavy work from beginning to end, come fine weather or foul - and in the North Yorkshire Moors there was plenty of foul.

In 1998 he had fallen from a roof, breaking his wrist, his knee, his collar bone and damaging his spine. He had been lucky to survive. Now his spine was giving him problems. The discs were crumbling at the base and this meant he was often in agony.

A consultant recommended an operation which would fuse the bottom few vertebrae and give Rob a chance of living with less pain. Without the operation the consultant thought it probable that Rob would eventually become unable to walk. He had little choice but to agree to the operation which meant a lengthy recuperation period. Luckily it could go ahead within a few weeks of the consultation. Rob finished all ongoing work and we prepared for the time ahead. First we decided it would be better for him to stay at Cat's Cradle. That way I could look after him while I worked from home. Bess the dog of course could come and live with us too. There was also the question of the pigeons. It would be difficult for me to drive down to Sleights to see to them twice a day when there were so many other things to do. We stood in the garden and measured the lawn. There was just room for the loft at the far edge by the fence but it meant taking the loft to pieces, transporting it to Rilldale and then rebuilding it in my garden.

Rob took on the task as though it was the job of a morning and recruited his friend Brian to help. Soon they had transported all the pieces of the shed to Rilldale and lifted them over the fence at the back of the garden. The pigeons were in baskets, fluttering and cooing in surprise at being ejected from their home. Rob and Brian managed to position the loft it so that it cast no shadows on my beautiful roses. After a day of hard work it stood in its new place with the pigeons locked inside. They needed a few weeks to adjust to their new home. If we let them out straight away they would fly back to Sleights and we'd have to start all over again. George the hen moved in with the pigeons, so that at last we had our bathroom back again.

Despite having all this new livestock outside, the house seemed empty. I missed the kittens tearing around the place, swinging from the curtains and scampering up and down the stairs play fighting with each other. I badly missed Gracie May's serenity and her soft warm fur as she sat under the hedge enjoying the sun. On the up side I had little Blaze all to myself. He would run around until he was exhausted then nod off to sleep against my neck or in the crook of my elbow, even though he was beginning to get a little too big to balance there safely.

During that summer Rob's girls both moved out of the house in Sleights to more independent and private lives. Rachel had moved up to the North East coast to a research job near Alnwick and Sarah had moved in with her boyfriend in Whitby. Now it began to feel like an indulgence to keep two houses running, not to mention the costs involved. We decided to spruce the place up and let it out. This would help us in the time ahead when Rob was recovering and seemed to make sense all round.

We found a tenant quickly. A friend's son and his partner moved in with their family. Rob said it was good to think of the house full of children's laughter once again. He had brought his own family up in the house and had many happy memories of long evenings around the fire, of visits from granny and grandpa and the table groaning with delicious food at tea time.

The time soon came for Rob to be admitted to hospital. Rob drove himself with me as a passenger, knowing it would be the last time he could drive for some time. We arrived just after dawn, where the industrial chimneys of Teesside were silhouetted against the fading red of the sky and we saw a couple of early dog walkers in the otherwise empty streets. We were shown into a ward and Rob unloaded his bag into the locker at the side of the bed. He got changed and climbed into bed as instructed and then there was nothing to do but leave him while he was prepared for theatre. It was still only seven o'clock. I wandered out into the grounds and looked up at the Rob's window. He was looking out at the same time and we waved to each other. He looked tiny and far away on the top floor of the building and I was so aware of his vulnerability. Time dragged. I sat in the café with a coffee, read a magazine and walked around the hospital corridors. Every now and then I would return to the ward but there was no sign of him. Hour after hour went by and I watched porters wheel other people back to comfortable places where they could come round slowly but there was no Rob. I had a long lunch in the canteen and still he hadn't returned. It took seven long hours of waiting before I saw him again. I heard the nurses speaking with each other as they wheeled him into a place by the window.

'Poor man, they've had a right old job with him.'

When they transferred him into bed Rob was overheated. His face was red and puffy and his eyes seemed sealed shut. Within ten minutes however he was awake and surprisingly alert, asking for water and holding my hand. After a few hours we learned that the surgeon had punctured his spinal cord while he had been operating and that was what had caused the delay. Rob would need to remain in hospital for two weeks while they made sure his spinal fluid levels were correct and that the cord had begun to heal properly. Luckily there had been no damage to the nerves but I understood that in these days of hasty discharges they must have had significant concern to keep him in so long for observation.

So began two weeks of visiting Rob every day. I took him supplies of food and baggy shorts which he requested in bright cheerful colours. These were the only clothing he felt

comfortable and cool in. I fed the pigeons and George the hen,
walked Bess, played with the tiny kitten and made sure that dog
and kitten were a safe distance from each other when I left the
house. Before he had gone in for his operation Rob had
constructed a wooden fence which kept Bess at one side of the
open plan kitchen/lounge area, he told me I would soon see why
he had done this. When we brought Bess to Cat's Cradle she
reacted to the kitten as though he was an old enemy. She growled
and barked and tried to bite him, narrowly missing his inquisitive
nose on a number of occasions. Rob explained that an adult cat
had badly scratched her when she had been a puppy and she had
never forgotten it. For her, all cats were potential bringers of
pain, and she wasn't going to be caught out twice.

When I left the house I had to lock the kitten in the bathroom and
leave Bess in the lounge to be sure that the kitten was out of
harm's way. Although Bess could not get into the lounge, the
kitten was small enough to wander into the kitchen where Bess
would be waiting for him.

In the moments I had to myself I resurrected an old passion of
mine, painting. I loved to work on big canvasses and used acrylic
paint on sponges, cloth, screwed up paper or even my hands to
get an abstract effect. I loved the colours of the peaty heathland,
the shades of stone and water and I spent many happy hours
working the paint across canvas after canvas. I missed Gracie
May a great deal and was so grateful for Bess's company. My
new little friend was a delight, the one with a black head and
white nose with the distinctive twin flames curling up his nose,

with his dainty front ankle socks and his back legs adorned with dazzling white stockings. His whiskers were a thick drooping white and Rob had nicknamed him Fu Manchu after the fictional evil genius, but there was nothing evil about this little kitty. I had called him Blaze because of the markings on his nose, but that was a lazy name and I knew it was likely he would earn a new more fitting one once he had shown us what sort of a cat he was.

I took some holiday leave. Each day I would lay my latest painting out to dry on the kitchen table while I travelled the hour or so to James Cook hospital to visit Rob. Later on I would take Bess out for her walk then work on my painting for a little longer. I painted as much for the process as the end result. I was painting away the pain I felt at Gracie's death, my worry about Rob and whether the operation would prove to be a success, my concern about how we would afford to live with only one income while Rob recovered and of course the worry about the house at Nancy Grove, which still did not have a buyer.

After I had finished painting I would listen to the radio. 'Desert island discs' on a Friday morning was a favourite. Sue Lawley presented the programme but came to the end of an almost twenty year reign with her interview of Joan Plowright in August of that year. I listened to the Dame, twenty eight years married to Laurence Olivier, talking about how she never lost sight of who she was in any relationship, how she always took a little nugget of herself everywhere she went. I nodded to myself, thinking how right she was and how Rob and I seemed to be managing to keep those nuggets of ourselves safe but at the same time loving every minute we spent together.

I relaxed in my favourite chair, which Rob had given to me. The chair had wings which were so enormous I felt they could shelter me from any storm. It was covered in buttery red leather, creased and glowing with age. Little Blaze would play at my feet, pounce on a scuttling spider, or leap onto the sofa and run around the sides like it was a wall of death, hanging on with needle-like claws. When he was exhausted he would clamber up my arm and fall asleep on my shoulder or in the crook of my arm, whistling softly. I had never heard a cat make this type of snoring sound before. All the cats I had known in the past were silent sleepers, but this one not only whistled but made tiny creaks and groans like a door in a gale.

One night I had a dream. I was walking along a shoreline on fairly solid ground when a large wave reared up. I knew it was going to break over my head but I didn't feel afraid. The wave did break, but somehow the water didn't have much weight. I was wet and uncomfortable but didn't lose my footing. I clenched my teeth which began to chatter and laughed because I knew I had escaped certain death. Someone was standing next to me and I shouted 'Run for it!' We ran to a shelter with dark caverns and looked out onto a night scene, with thunder cracking and lightening streaking across the sky. We had reached safety before the storm broke and turned to each other with smiles of relief. Our clothes were dry.

The next morning I had an offer on the house. A landlord wanted it to add to his portfolio and was prepared to pay just over £52,000. It marked the end of my Nancy Grove adventure, although in reality it had been much more of a misadventure. If it hadn't have been for the rising market I would have lost money I could ill afford to lose. Instead, after the work I had paid for on the house and taxes I had made about £8000. It was a salutary lesson in listening to the advice of others who knew better. It brought to mind the old song – 'Fools rush in, where angels fear to tread.' I told Rob about the offer while he was in hospital.

'I've been very lucky,' I said

'Well, it's better to try these things than regret not having given it a go,' he said, and squeezed my hand.

Rob was an outdoor man forced to lie in a warm ward and his hands, feet and face had swelled up in the heat. He was always in good spirits despite his obvious pain and he cheered everyone up with the sight of his comical brightly patterned baggy shorts as he lay on top of the bedcovers. The nurses pretended to put on their sun glasses to dim the glare when they arrived at his bedside and before long they realised he was a person they could have a bit of banter with. Several of them also asked him for advice on their do- it -yourself projects. His swollen face made him look like a wise old Buddha.

One day I arrived home tired and a little tearful. The ward manager had told us that Rob's spinal cord was not healing as it should and that he would need to spend longer in hospital and I felt lonelier than the first time I had walked across the threshold of Cat's Cradle. I heard the tags clink on Bess's collar as she got to her feet in the growing gloom of the kitchen and I saw the outline of her tail wagging in the fading light. Beyond Bess I saw a thin crescent moon skeined with cloud, balanced on the horizon like a huge question mark. I had hoped I could begin to look after Rob at home, but it looked as though we would have to hang on just a little longer.

I left the lights off to enjoy that pale moonlight, took Bess's lead from its hook and heard the sharp click as it fastened on. I spoke to her quietly, her wet nose enquiring upwards as she snorted softly in anticipation of the walk ahead, then I turned on the outside light so that we would see our way back into the house in the darkness. As I walked out of the village bats flitted, a lone sheep bleated out on the moor, moonlight marbled the low cloud and over the sound of Bess's breathing I could hear the river far away down in the valley. I felt peaceful and for more than the first time in my life I had a sense of walking side by side with something I found difficult to describe, but it was something warm and benevolent and helped to make life seem better. In that moment I knew that I wasn't really alone, that I never had been alone, and that I never would be alone for the rest of my life.

I returned to the house and broke the spell of darkness with electric light. Then I saw that the door to the stairs was open. I called up to the next floor 'Kitty, kitty?' but there was no answering mew. I climbed to the top of the stairs. No kitten. At the bottom of the stairs I peered into the kitchen, it was only then that I noticed that the painting I had laid out to dry earlier in the day had been knocked to the floor. Across the soft contoured strokes of burnt umber, raw sienna and graphite grey was a glorious angular streak of cerulean blue with two blots of deep black by its side. Tubes of paint lay on the kitchen floor and paint was on the carpet. The newspaper which I had placed under the drying painting was spread unevenly under the table, one sheet was torn and a section was screwed up like a concertina where a paw had landed and skidded off. I was looking at the aftermath of a cat and dog chase. Bess had been constrained within the kitchen, but the kitten had not. Eventually I found my secret Picasso - there behind the flap of the sofa, covered in paint the colour of heathland but with one dramatic exception - the pads of his back paws had been transformed from salmon pink to a brilliant cerulean blue. From that moment he had a new name – Pablo Picasso, and within a short time it was as though he'd never had any other.

Chapter 19

Rob and I received the news he could come home one happy day
at the beginning of September. A physiotherapist came out to th
house and arranged to have a grab rail fitted to the side of the be
so he could pull himself up while his wounds healed. He had to
rest for long periods of time and we acquired a second hand
television from a friend with an integrated DVD player, so that
Rob could entertain himself during the long days when I needed
to work. He didn't sleep well and I would sometimes wake up ir
the night to see the ghostly glare of Open University programme
on the screen with Rob sitting up in bed wearing earphones. We
hadn't bothered with a television until then. We had never felt
the need for it and would always rather pick up a book or listen
to music. However, we became firm fans of the programme
'Homes under the Hammer' during that autumn. We were so
relieved that our property drama was at an end, it was a guilty
pleasure to listen to the ups and downs of other people's propert
adventures. Of course, I still had the house at Dellon Street. This
was still occupied by the same family who had moved in as soor
as it was bought. The rent rolled in and it was no trouble to
manage.

Pablo Picasso was growing bigger and stronger every day. His
blue eyes turned to cadmium green and he began to look sturdier
Bess could not get used to a kitten about the place and never let
up with her attempts to chase him, but Pablo was fast and Bess
was getting older. Her reactions were not what they had been.
She was now ten years old. Her hearing was not so good, and he

sight had lost its edge. Pablo would approach Bess one step at a time, as though he were a child playing the school game 'what time is it Mr Wolf?' then just as Bess made her lunge, Pablo would dart away, his tiny pipe cleaner tail held high in triumph.

Two of Pablo's brothers had only moved a few doors away, and we visited them to find out how they were getting along. Charlie and Ginger were in good condition. I remembered first seeing Ginger that day in Hull as he emerged from a pile of newspaper and thinking he had all the makings of a big ugly Tom cat. He had been all head with a tiny body. Now his body had caught up and he was a handsome, well- proportioned kitten. His colouring had changed from a dark streaky ginger to a delicate light marmalade colour. Charlie, the other black and white kitten, who was covered in a pattern like ink blots, was bigger than Pablo but less bold. Ginger led Charlie into danger and often got him into places he couldn't easily get out of, such as down the back of the sofa, or behind the kitchen units.

Charlie and Ginger's new owners left their new pets with us for a week while they went on holiday. This was a perfect solution for kittens that were too small to be left at a cattery and who were not yet old enough to go outside. Bess went almost insane with frustration. She must have thought she was seeing treble. Everywhere she looked there were kittens. She was stuck in the lower part of the house with a constant barrier to her sinking her teeth into three balls of leaping, pouncing, spring loaded fur. Thankfully she rarely barked, but would lunge at the fence then look at me as though I were the least understanding person in the world. When they had exhausted themselves I would wonder where the kittens had gone, but when I went upstairs with a tray for Rob's meal I would often find them sleeping all together in a heap on his chest.

One cool September morning I lit the wood burning stove for the first time that year. I tightly crumpled four or five sheets of newspaper, then added chopped sticks in the shape of a wigwam, and set a match to it. I enjoyed that first scent of burning paper, and the scorched smell of the dust inside the heating chimney. As the sticks took hold I added oval pieces of compressed coal, and watched as they began to splutter then glow. I closed up the glass and watched as the fire began to roar. The stove stood proud of the wall with a pipe leaving the back and leading up to the chimney. On the top of it was a flat plate, perfect for simmering winter stews. In fact once the fire got going the whole of the casing would radiate with heat. That was one of the reasons the room was so much warmer than when I had the open fire. The open fire lost most of its heat up the chimney, but with the burner, the heat stayed in the room.

The kittens had watched in fascination as I had set the fire and they now stood transfixed in front of it so that I could see miniature flames reflected in their eyes. Charlie and Pablo had spent a good half an hour chasing each other around the room; they had been to the top of the curtain, had balanced on the thin edge of a draw, had wriggled underneath the dresser and to my shame had come out sneezing, covered with cobwebs. Now they were ready for a rest. They lay down in front of the fire relaxing in the warmth, uncoiling like spent springs, their tiny bellies exposed to the heat. Ginger had been on a mission around the chair cushions, patting at them and exploring them using his nose and paws to feel underneath. He had escaped Bess's desperate attempt to clamp her jaws around his tail and was now beginning to wind himself up to a circuit around the walls. He began by leaping on the spot. He went straight up into the air a couple of feet and came down facing the opposite way, his fur on end and his back arched. Then he jumped about the room as though he were made out of rubber, displacing papers and pens, books and ornaments. Next he began to jump from chair to chair and round and round in a frenzy. Suddenly he veered off course and included the hot plate of the wood burner as a launch pad. His paws made a quick sizzling sound like bacon hitting the pan. Before I had chance to shriek he had leapt off again soundlessly. Too shocked to even cry out he dashed behind a curtain and cowered, lifting his paws up and down in agony.

I ran to the kitchen and filled a bowl with cold water. Can you imagine trying to get an eight week old kitten with burnt paws to stand in a bowl of cold water? Ginger yowled and struggled but I got the better of him. The pads on two of his feet were red and scorched, though there were no blisters. Thankfully his reflexes were good and he had jumped away from danger before any serious damage could be done. I locked Pablo and Charlie upstairs and took Ginger 'hot foot' to the vet. Simon gave me cream to soothe Ginger's burns and he returned with his paw pads slathered in a Vaseline type goo which he immediately licked off.

He never jumped on the fire plate again.

## Chapter 20

Alison, the letting agent gave me a call. Our tenants in Dellon Street had decided to move house and after three happy years of pain free letting it was time to place the house up for rent again. Rob and I discussed whether this was really what we wanted to do. I would need to travel through to Hull on my own to freshen the place up and prepare it for a new family. Rob would be out of action for a matter of months, perhaps longer and if there were any problems with the house in the near future I would need to rely on local Hull builders. Although my experience with Mr Apollo had not been a complete disaster, I had got so used to the way Rob worked I really didn't want to get used to anyone else. Perhaps now was the time to think of ending my buy to let experience altogether and concentrate on helping Rob to get better. We both agreed this was the best thing to do. Once the tenant had moved out I checked the place over, painted the lounge, tidied the yard and called the estate agent which had dealt with Nancy Grove for a valuation.

After a few days of chill, the September weather returned to the heat of mid-summer. The temperature often hovered around 22 degrees centigrade and the trees, unmolested by wind or storm developed touches of gold among the deep green. Ginger and Charlie had returned home after their holiday stay and it felt very quiet with only Bess and Pablo around. Thankfully the kittens' new owners were very understanding about Ginger's burns and I sent him home with the tube of ointment for his healing pads.

One morning I was aware of a thundering sound and went to the bottom of the garden to look out over the field. A small herd of black and white bullocks had been released and were racing around all together, snorting and kicking. A neighbour's black cat streaked across the grass from among the massive roots of the solitary oak where she had been watching for rabbits and slid under the fence away from the galloping hooves. The bullocks slowed down and trotted joyfully around with their tails held high, looking over their new terrain. The roses in my garden were blossoming like midsummer and they released their scent into the air as I walked past them to get to the commotion. After a few minutes the bullocks came over to meet me, pushing their noses up towards my hands and rolling their great eyes in surprise as I patted their warm coats.

The lawn was a tired green from lack of water, the baskets looked weary and the yew hedge was overgrown and spreading out onto the patio. I had neglected everything while I had been travelling back and forth to the hospital, but now Rob was home I really needed to get on top of general maintenance jobs again. For the time being, everything was down to me. As it was such a beautiful day I decided to cut the grass, water the drooping baskets and trim the hedge. By coffee time I had a bin liner full of clippings and the hedge was back in line. I had trimmed back some really thick branches and sawed these into short logs to set by the fire to dry. I knew that yew was poisonous to horses, and that they would happily eat it even though it had fatal consequences. Horses and cattle were one thing, but Pablo ate ca meat and drank milk. I had never seen him attempt to eat anything green and since Ginger had burnt his paw pads on the fire Pablo never seemed to venture anywhere near the wood burner where I had stacked the yew logs, so I had no worries. I was pleased at the sight of the logs stored in readiness for the cooler weather to come.

Without any further thought I got changed and drove down to the Coop for the weekly shop. This was Whitby's only supermarket, situated near the railway station and right in the centre of all the hustle and bustle. Seagulls wheeled over my head and families walked about with ice creams, enjoying the unseasonably warm weather. I saw an old school friend and stood for a while catching up on news. Little did I know that precious seconds were ticking away and that back home a small black and white kitten desperately needed my help.

When I returned from shopping I unloaded the car in a leisurely way. I shouted a hello up the stairs to Rob and put the kettle on to make us a brew. Pablo was playing with a pigeon feather which had wafted in from the shed and Bess was mooching about the kitchen looking for scraps. When I had put away the tins and packets I went to straighten the rug in front of the fire. It was then that I noticed the yew logs and the signs of tiny teeth marks on one of them. There were a couple of short branches with yew leaves which also showed the imprint of sharp teeth. I picked up the log and turned it around in my hand. Pablo had chewed all around the circumference and there were splinters where he had pulled at the bark.

'Is yew poisonous to cats?' I asked Rob, hurriedly handing him his cup of tea in bed.

'I think it's poisonous to all animals,' he said

'I need to phone the vet,' I had that terrible numb feeling of panic I remembered so well from Nancy Grove. I had invested so much time and love in this tiny ball of fur that I could barely hold the telephone to make the call. I held Pablo on my knee while I spoke to Simon the vet. I looked at my lovely kitten closely before fastening him into his carrier but there were no signs of discomfort. He sat there contentedly looking at me as if to say. 'What's the adventure?'

The drive to the vet's seemed to take forever, although it was only twenty minutes. As soon as I arrived the veterinary nurse ushered me past the waiting queue directly to the vet.

My mouth felt dry and my throat began to close. I couldn't believe after all the dangers we had avoided in his short few weeks on earth that Pablo's life was in danger again.

'I know it sounds harsh, but he's not a special breed. If the worst comes to the worst we have other kittens here looking for homes.'

He may not have been a special breed, but Pablo Picasso was very special to me. After the death of Gracie May I had become ever more attached to this bundle of affection.

At home after the danger was over I watched him fall into a healing sleep with a sense of gratitude and relief.

After the yew episode Pablo continued to torment me by placing his life in danger. One evening I came home from work late. It was dark and Rob had made his way downstairs to sit in a chair to read the paper by lamplight and the glow of the fire. He had his feet up and it was good to see him smiling and looking stronger. When Rob was well and working hard, he expended a huge amount of energy. He would come home, run a bath to wash off the day's hard toil and needed to stock up on food well before his evening meal. These were his Scooby Snacks, named after the cartoon character Scooby Doo's famous eating habits. For any normal person these would be more than a dinner in themselves, but for Rob they just kept him going until he could get his teeth into steak and kidney pudding or chicken stew. He might take a pile of crackers and cheese, a slice of left over pie, an orange, a packet of Jaffa cakes, and a few after eight mints all balanced on a plate into the bathroom with him and eat them with a mug of tea while he soaked in the water. Friends were amazed at the amount of food he could put away, yet he remained lean because he used up every calorie of energy he consumed.

While he recuperated these Scooby Snacks were less extravagant and on this evening Rob had only a chicken leg, a packet of crisps, half a dozen tomatoes, a piece of cucumber sliced into long batons, a hunk of last year's Christmas cake and the best part of a jar of peanut butter which he ate on its own from a desert spoon.

'I've run the bath for you,' he said as I came through the door. 'Tea's in the oven and will be ready when you come out.'

When I went into the bathroom the scent of lavender bubble bath drifted up from the water and a candle burned at the end of the tub, the light from its flame reflected in the mirror and cast flickering shadows around the room. It was just what I needed. Within a couple of minutes I was luxuriating in the warmth, up to my neck in lavender bubbles. Pablo pushed the door open and padded across to see what was going on. He jumped up onto the side of the bath and walked up and down the edge for a while, peering into the water as though he would discover his future in it. He reached out a tentative paw and patted the surface, then lowered his face and sneezed when the bubbles burst on his nose. Next, he settled himself half in and half out of the water balanced on the top of my chest just under my chin and fell asleep. He stayed like this for a good twenty minutes, even returning to his post after I had reached over to top up the hot water.

When I climbed out I placed Pablo onto the floor, dried myself, pulled the plug and wandered into the bedroom to put on something warm, taking Pablo with me. The bath water usually emptied quickly and quietly but this time it was making a strange noise so I went back to investigate. I turned on the light to see that Pablo had dashed back to the bathroom and was balanced on the edge of the bath. The plug had partially replaced itself and the water was slowly dragging past it making a squealing sound. Before I had chance to do anything, Pablo had leapt into the bath, his little legs outstretched as though he expected to skate across the surface like a water beetle. He plunged in like a bundle of rags, and quickly began to sink down, his black and white fur streaming out behind him. He had reached the bottom of the bath before I had covered the four steps to get to him. I reached in and scooped him out expecting a coughing, spluttering, distressed little kitten to come out in my hands, but there was none of that. Pablo submitted to my vigorous drying, shook himself, licked himself a few times and then without a backward glance trotted off to see what other mischief he could get himself into. Not for the first time I realised I was going to need to develop nerves of steel if I was to survive the troubles of being a proxy mother to this bold little kitten.

## Chapter 21

Winter came early. After a long warm autumn, a sudden icy win
came in from the north and blasted most of the leaves from the
trees in one weekend. Great drifts of wet leaves were flattened
against walls and clogged the rivers. One morning just after
dawn in late November I drove my trusty car up out of Grosmon
village, towards the moor road. I had spent a quarter of an hour
scraping ice from the windscreen in sleet to prepare for my
journey to work in Beadling.  Now I made my way though Egto
and down into Grosmont, and the steam railway made famous b
the Harry Potter films. Near Grosmont, in the village of
Goathland, Harry Potter had alighted on his journey to Hogwart
School of Wizardry. Unlike Mr Potter I had no moving
staircases, nor messenger owls to look forward to, but a grim
visit to a cold office to check paperwork.

The gates were closed at the level crossing in Grosmont and I
watched the huge pistons of a blue steam engine power past me
with plumes of white steam billowing up into an indigo sky.
Black tarmac glistened and a rail worker walked out of the gloo
wearing a yellow oilskin, head down against the icy squalls.
Once the gates had opened I drove up the steep road towards
Fairhead and further up to the cattle crossing that marked the
beginning of the lonely ribbon of road to Beadling. The sleet he
gave way to snow, which fell like an explosion of feathers acros
the windscreen. In the car headlights the flakes swirled and
danced towards me. Within five minutes the road was covered
and as I climbed higher still I felt the tyres slip on ice. I saw

headlights coming down towards me. The advancing car was inching ominously closer, sliding sideways at times, the wipers working furiously and a great overhang of snow was sliding from the roof towards the windscreen. There were no passing places, but I pulled as far in as I could to let them past. The passenger raised her arm and wagged a finger, as if to say don't go any further. I didn't need a second warning. This was the road that had blocked the day I had moved to Rilldale. The snowploughs had thrown a wall of snow into the turning which made it impossible for even a four wheel drive vehicle to negotiate. Turning round was more of a problem. I backed fifty yards down to the cattle grid where there was the entrance to a quarry and managed a slithering three point turn.

In Rilldale the snow was lying on the road and the tyre tracks were quickly filling with a fresh layer of white. Pablo was inside the house looking out at the snow through the patio windows. His breath had fogged the glass and I could see where it had condensed into droplets as he had moved along to keep a clear view. The solitary oak had disappeared behind the swirling whiteness and it was difficult to see any further than the end of the garden.

I settled down to complete paperwork at home and sent e mails to let people know where I was. I took a photograph of the great white blotches falling in a black and white world and sent it to colleagues. One who lived in the milder climate of York e mailed me back. 'When was this taken?' 'About five minutes ago.' I replied. 'Can't have, it is bright sunshine here!' she replied. It didn't matter how often I explained to people the difference in the weather between the flatter vale of York and the higher, more rugged North Yorkshire Moors, the reality rarely sunk in. A photo could convey what a thousand words could not.

Pablo jumped on my knee while I was writing and had soon curled up and gone to sleep. I had phone calls to make and I wondered if the people on the other end of the phone could hear the wheezing and whistling noises from Pablo and if so, did they think it was me? Later, the snow stopped and the clouds broke. I took a mug of tea into the garden and looked in awe at the world of shimmering whiteness. There was a covering of four inches of snow everywhere and as the sun warmed the roof of the coal house the load began to slip from the top, revealing the startling orange of tiles. Pablo came to the door, yawning and stretching his legs, then sat quite still with his whiskers twitching. He was just over four months old and had grown into a long- legged slender young cat. Soon his paw prints had followed in the tracks of my wellingtons and we stood side by side taking in the wonder of it all.

I had been letting Pablo go out during the day time. After his injections he was safe to associate with other cats outside his immediate family and so was free to roam around the area of the house, always coming home before dark. I had recently bought him a bright red reflective collar with a bell to warn any small creatures of his approach and he looked splendidly smart in it. Simon the vet told me that cats regulated their own territory according to the strength of their personality and the number of other cats in the neighbourhood. As we were in a rural area there were miles of open fields and woods for Pablo to explore with territories to battle over. Right now however, he seemed content to restrict his wanderings to the field and the house where Ginger and Charlie lived. He would sometimes pay them a visit and keep them company for a while before coming home. Occasionally I would come across him while I was out for a walk and then he would run towards me like a long lost friend, mewing and rubbing himself against my leg. He would be happy to accompany me a little way along my favourite path, but after a short distance he would slow his pace and turn for home.

That afternoon Pablo went off on one of his explorations. The world seemed very bright and new to him and he looked around him with his eyes stretched wide with surprise. He jumped up onto the fence, knocking off the snow that had settled on the heavy post, then he made an enormous leap into the field, where the snow had drifted in places to approaching a foot deep. He sank down up to his belly and began to make great leaps over the mounds of covered dead grass and mole hills. He rolled and flicked showers of ice crystals into the air, snorted, licked the compacted snow from his fur, leapt again like a lamb on all fours and then disappeared into the garden next door.

When it began to get dark I went out to the garden and shouted softly for him. Usually I would hear a clear mewing from nearby and a black and white streak would come towards me. I waited as a lonely crow cawed from the wood and beyond that I heard the muted roar of the river. A blackbird regarded me with a wary eye from the bird table but there was no answering mew. An hour later I went out again. Shouted. Still no reply. I phoned Charlie and George's house. Their owner told me they were curled up in front of the fire, but no Pablo kept them company. Just before bed time I walked up towards the Institute and hung over a gate, straining my eyes in the darkness to see if there was a familiar shape down by the oak or at the edge of the field before the wood. Nothing.

Rob was philosophical and urged me not to worry. Eventually every cat has the instinct to stay out in the night. There are sights sounds and scents which call to them from the fields and they need to follow them. I should relax and trust that he would come home soon, probably in the middle of the night, but at least by morning. I knew Rob was right. I had no desire to keep Pablo locked inside and give him a half- life of pampered protection. I wanted him to be free and with that I knew came danger and uncertainty- but why couldn't he have chosen a warmer night? I worried about him out in the snow, visible against the whiteness, prey to bigger cats and possibly foxes.

I woke at about four in the morning to the sound of wind moaning down the chimney and felt sure Pablo would be on a chair somewhere asleep. I put on my dressing gown and crept downstairs to check. The last embers were still glowing in the wood burning stove and the room was warm, but Pablo was nowhere to be seen. I looked towards the patio doors and saw snow plastered against the lower portion of glass, driven there by fresh showers and wind. When I tried to open the door it was frozen shut. I pulled hard and eventually the ice gave and a freezing gust of wind blew inside. I shouted out into the night. No faint mew in the distance. No furry body rubbing against my leg. I went back up to bed and slept fitfully until dawn.

Eventually a thin grey light filtered through the bedroom windows. Outside, a barn owl hooted mournfully and beat away into the woodland. I pulled on my wellingtons and walked across the field into the wood calling out from time to time in the hope that Pablo would somehow have survived the wintery night. A single deer looked up then silently white tailed away between the trees. Holly berries, torn from the branches by the wind were strewn across the snow like blood. I heard a rustling and rushed over to see a blackbird among the twigs under a canopy of pine. Slowly I trudged home. I pushed the cat flap dejectedly, checking for the tenth time that we hadn't locked it by mistake. It swung back and forth freely, each time making the noise I longed to hear as it clicked open. Later I walked down to the shop and asked if anyone had mentioned finding a young cat, but nobody had. Back at home I found a recent photograph of Pablo and stuck it to a card with my phone number. Lynn in the shop put it in the window for me. On my way back home I passed a couple of people I knew and asked them to look out for him. I looked across the road and tried to peer in people's gardens. It was no use. Pablo had completely disappeared. As the day wore on I imagined him locked in someone's shed, cold and afraid, or worse, dead behind some hedge or in the river.

The day dragged hopelessly on. The house seemed to echo and all the light had gone out of it. I took Bess out for her walk and we slipped and slid up the street. Even she seemed subdued and couldn't wait to turn for home. It remained dull and cold, with a slow wet thaw that melted everything to slush. By three o'clock the sky was beginning to darken again and still there was no sign I had to accept I would be spending another night without my little cat. Rob curled up in bed asleep while I lay staring at the ceiling, my ears straining, willing myself to hear the sound of tiny paws on the stairs. But save for the wind which began to blow again and the creaking of the house, the rest was silence.

After a few days I began to believe that Pablo had met some predator, or in his youthful enthusiasm he had wandered too far and been overcome by the cold. I had trouble sleeping. One night a book fell from the bedside table and in my half sleep it felt like the weight of a little cat jumping onto the bed. I visited Charlie and Ginger who had the sense to stay indoors and their owner told me that Pablo had stopped visiting them the day he had gone missing from home. The difficult thing was not knowing what had happened to him. I pictured all sorts of horrible situations, the worst of which involved him being trapped somewhere nearby and starving slowly to death. Every day I went out and looked for him. I asked people I didn't know to look in their outbuildings.

One person told me they had seen a dead cat up by the farm, run over by a tractor and moved to the side of the road. They said it was young, and that it was black and white. With a heavy heart I walked up the lane, found the place and looked down on the matted body of a farm cat. It wasn't my Pablo. I was relieved, though the sight of the poor thing lying there in a snowy grave was so sad.

As we moved into the third week I realised that I was going to have to get on with my life. Pablo was gone and there was nothing I could do. If he had become stuck somewhere it was unlikely he would have survived the three weeks since his disappearance. Nobody could give me a clue as to what had happened to him, it was as though he had jumped through the hedge and into a parallel universe.

Twenty two days after I last saw my little cat, I received a call from the estate agent telling me that the house on Dellon street had sold. My Hull experience was drawing to a close.

That afternoon I was walking up the road after telling Lynn the shop keeper my good news when a woman who worked as a home help stopped me. I had seen her a couple of times pulling up to a house at the top of the village wearing her blue uniform. She looked smart and business- like.

'I'm Joyce's carer, Susan, I visit her every day,' she said.

'Who do you mean?' I asked. I knew most of the people in this part of the village but had never heard of anyone called Joyce.

'She has early dementia and is very lame. I need to pop in to make sure she hasn't blown herself up with the cooker. But she has a good routine and she manages quite well with the help we give her. She's such a great character, full of stories. Anyway, I've just started to work for this organisation and I got my instructions about what I need to do for Joyce but they never mentioned the cat.'

'What cat?' I said.

'Well, the first morning I visited Joyce It had been a terrible night and I could see she had been out for more coal because she had left the coal house door open. How she managed to get out there without killing herself I can't imagine. Anyway, before I left I asked her if there was anything else she wanted me to do, and she told me to feed the cat. Then I noticed this black and white ball of fur, quite young, asleep on the sofa. I thought, what fool gave her a cat when she finds it so difficult to look after herself?'

'So what did you do?' I asked

'Well I kept feeding it. She called it Thomas. I bought cat biscuits and fed him on left- over meat and he had a dollop of cream every now and then, I even bought him a litter tray because I could see she hadn't one. She told me she never let him out. Then I saw your poster in the shop window.'

'Do you think he could be Pablo?' I said, a tiny bird of hope stirring in my chest.

'Well that's the funny thing. The regular home help, Betty, went to Australia to visit her family and when she got back yesterday she called in and asked where the cat had come from. You see, Joyce did have a cat called Thomas, but Betty told me that was way back when her kids were young. Those kids have grown up children of their own now so I think this cat could be yours.'

Susan and I walked together to where Joyce lived. Susan let herself in and there sitting in an old wing backed chair by the fire was Joyce. In the chair opposite sat Pablo Picasso. Bigger than I remembered and fatter, fed on cream and best meat and pampered by Joyce who though he belonged to her.

Pablo looked up and gave a short 'mew' of recognition. He yawned, stretched and clambered off his chair to wind himself around my legs. Joyce eyed me with suspicion.

After the introductions and chat about the weather I told her I too had a cat, and that he had gone missing. Joyce shook her head in sympathy. After a few more minutes I ventured a casual query. 'Do you think this really is your Thomas?' and bent down to pick Pablo up. He turned to plant a wet lick on the side of my face.

'You see, I think he might just be my cat Pablo.'

Joyce's reached out her arms to examine her Thomas again, a frown of uncertainty gathering on her brow.

'Do you remember Joyce, you did have a cat but that was a little time ago?' said Susan.

Joyce tickled Pablo under the chin with a gnarled finger and began to nod.

"My Thomas was just like this one, but his paws were black. I remember now, he died in the snow of '61,' she said, stroking Pablo's head, tears forming in her old blue eyes. I sat beside her and patted her arm. Susan put the kettle on.

'I'm sure he will come to visit you.' I said later. We had finished a large pot of strong tea served from gold rimmed cups and had each polished off a toasted tea cake which Susan had smothered with butter and strawberry jam. I knew that neither I nor Pablo could resist the call of Joyce's treats for long.

'You take him on condition you come back soon for a cuppa,' she said and I nodded. 'Of course I will'.

I looked forward to popping in on Joyce again. When I did I realised she had long moments of clarity where she entertained us with stories about the old days. She told us about the great snow of 1947 when the drifts formed a tunnel at Lythe bank and traffic drove through a curve of whiteness. She let out a mischievous cackle when she told us about stealing the boy's clothes as they washed in the river. Her sweetheart had died of tuberculosis when she was twenty three and there had never been anyone else after that. She had turned down a local farmer, though everyone advised her to take his offer of a secure home. She had money enough to live in modest comfort and this is what she had done. She blew her nose on a large white handkerchief when we got up to leave and I could see she was sad to have lost her new feline friend but I was also so relieved that the truant Pablo was found.

Joyce walked out of her back door in December to get coal for the fire, even though the home help had left her with plenty to last her through the day. The ice had made a treacherous skating rink of her yard and she lost her footing and fell by the coal house door. A passer-by found her covered in coal dust crying out in pain and she was rushed into hospital where they discovered she had broken her hip. I went to visit her, but she didn't recognise me. All I could do was to hold her hand. She was in a poor way, her broken hip had caused complications and she developed a blood clot.

She passed away three days before Christmas with her old home help Betty at her bedside. They told me she had not been in pain and I was glad that she had not suffered for long. I found Pablo outside her door as I was taking Bess for her afternoon stroll and he was looking up at the door handle as though expecting Joyce to open it and invite him in for more juicy meat or a dollop of cream.

## Chapter 22

Rob and I went out a few days before Christmas and bought a live tree, which we took home and placed proudly in a corner of the room where it could peer out towards the majestic snow-capped trees at the end of the field. We hung it with lights and glittering baubles, home-made paper chains and parcels tied with ribbon and heaped up our presents in a nest of tinsel. This Christmas the stove burned brightly, the candles glowed and the cottage filled with the warm scent of cinnamon and cloves as we prepared traditional Christmas punch.

On Christmas Eve I shut Pablo upstairs both to keep him safe and to save Bess's sanity. Whenever Pablo went anywhere near the kitchen which was now Bess's domain, she would growl and try to snap at him. Sometimes I worried that Pablo left his retreat a little too late, and that it would take only a split second of mistiming for Bess's impressively sharp teeth to close around his fragile throat.

Rob and I crunched on frozen snow down the village to a neighbour's house for mulled wine and mince pies. I was so glad I had made the decision to move to Rilldale, I already felt I had lived there for years and everyone was so friendly. When we stepped back out of our friend's house into the snow at around midnight the sky was scattered with stars which shone down bright and clear. A dog fox barked far away which made us only more aware of the stillness. We heard a metallic clink and saw our near neighbour fitting the key into the lock of his home. It was so late and so silent that we whispered our goodnights.

When we arrived home I saw that the barrier between the kitchen and the lounge was no longer in place and that Bess was fast asleep in front of the fire. The door to the stairs was swinging open which could only mean that Pablo Picasso was loose somewhere. Perhaps we had walked into the aftermath of another race around the house, if so, they had both carefully avoided upsetting the tree or any ornaments. I called to Pablo softly, hoping not to disturb Bess who looked so comfortable in her dream world.

I turned on the main light so that I could search for him better. Bess lay on her side with her legs out in front of her and her head thrown back a little. Her black sides rose and fell rhythmically with her breathing. She stirred and sighed and then she opened her eyes. I could see she understood that something was unusual and I braced myself to jump to the rescue, but Bess just sighed again and stretched her back towards a shape pressed up against her as she drifted back off to sleep. And there, nestled in her neck fur, stretched his length and purring loudly, was a very fine black and white cat, with front paws as white as washing and back legs dressed in snowy stockings. His white, Fu Manchu whiskers drooped downwards towards the rug and twin flames of white curled upwards between his gently closed eyes.

Pablo Picasso.

## About the Author

 Karen Ritson trained as a teacher, social worker, and more recently as a massage therapist. She loves long country walks, jazz music and photography. Karen is a regular contributor to the local Valley News magazine and won the York St John University travel writing competition whilst completing a Master of Arts in 2011.

She lives in a small village in North Yorkshire with her cat, Pablo Picasso, and her partner Rob.

9 780993 451003